TOMORROW STOLE TODAY

A COLLECTION OF DAILY POETRY

Alexander Schotten

of the Lifted Poets Society

Copyright © 2023 Alexander Schotten

All rights reserved.

ISBN: **9798853844407**

DEDICATION

To Bravo,
The best cat a guy could ask for
"Joy is sorrow unmasked"

Preface

    Poetry saved my life well before I understood it needed saving. I've always loved words, as a kid I wouldn't eat dinner without a Harry Potter book present, with the grease stains as evidence across all seven books. I always felt my brain processed everything & reacted through some sort of auto pilot. Then later after I read, & eventually wrote, I'd be able to replay the scenes of the day & all the cue's I missed before were obvious. The character development was emphasized & the ending predictable. I would stew over the fact that I couldn't find the same peace in social settings that I found with literature, especially when I thoroughly enjoyed all the activities I was involved in.

    As the years progressed in the experiment of life, the variables increased. One of which was a crippling addiction to finding that peace in the strongest, most convenient & quickest route possible. For myself, that was opiates, an easy cure to all my problems today (until tomorrow). Without getting too much into that (I think it deserves its own collection), it's important to acknowledge that the trauma derived from a lifestyle filled with emotional, mental & physical deterioration creates the perfect storm for someone struggling like I described above.

    So I met a problem that seems clear to everyone else, yet foggy to me. Like I was the only one at the sauna who didn't take off my sunglasses. Continue living a life of total destruction until I meet an inevitable death or buckle up & search for peace in other areas that would take time & patience. I chose death, for almost 7 years, which brought me across multiple states, some wild situations, a lot of run down hotels & eventually prison.

    Through all this poetry would shine like the sun directly in my eyes as I called it the moon. I'd find myself dope sick in a cell writing poems on the back of a jail handbook, or 30 days clean in a halfway house on the beach, or on the top of some mountain, homeless, trying to figure out if the shadows are creatures ready to attack or hallucinations from not sleeping. I can pinpoint prickles of peace scattered about my timeline & they directly correlate to whether there was a pencil in my hand or not, whether I was practicing recovery or death.

    Eventually, in prison, I'd come to the first realization of my ability to successfully process my emotions through writing. A period of my life where I was surrounded by trauma was overtly calm & content because I spent every moment I wasn't physically active, writing. The light switch hadn't been turned on yet, but there was a flicker in the bulb & with a little help from an electrician the wiring could be rerouted.

    Following prison, without drugs, I learned I could abuse peace in other forms that weren't as effective as narcotics but also held less consequences. So I let poetry smack me in the head, begging for attention through alcohol abuse, love, heartbreak, death & life, leaving behind crumbs of peace for my soul to grudgingly chase. Again I found myself choosing wrong over right justified by the wrong not being as wrong as my old lifestyle, until eventually I had worked, drank & loved my way into a state of physical & mental despair.

    This brings us up to March of 2022, a good friend who had read some of my poetry suggested I gather everything I had, through prisons, treatment, state to state, up until the present day & publish it. I'd spent months off the booze, intentionally writing, mirroring prison. I observed my thoughts, feelings & how I physically felt, then I brought it all to my therapist as if I were a scientist on the verge of cracking the code to Quantum Gravity. I felt like I was so close to finding the answer to the question I'd fallen asleep thinking about since I could remember.

    So join me here with my answer to my internal life's work. This book is the opposite of fundamentally sound, I did not care about proper formatting while I was regurgitating my soul into steel toilets and I did my best to not alter any of my original works unless I felt absolutely necessary. My suggestion is read this how I wrote it, edited it & still absorb it; grab yourself a cup of coffee, a fluffy pet & some headphones, throw on some melodic guitar riffs, and intentionally draw whatever reason you can from yourself to elicit whatever response feels right for the day. I know it's cliche, & if you know me personally you know I live by them, but this shared experience through art is far more important than we give credit.

With that being said, I also invite you to join me outside of the confines of these pages & into the new real world of social media (www.liftedpoetssociety.com), through an interactive blog where, hopefully, we can all share some of the same reasoning we get through art on a daily basis. You can also disregard all of this & fly through or return it before it's too late, my feelings won't be hurt. This first collection was selfishly, for me. Through all these words I was able to, at times, stay just present enough to stay alive & in others, the focus on now through poetry was the catalyst to life changing decisions. I hope my analogies, ironies & metaphors give you some of the same clarity as they give me.

CONTENTS

1	January	8
2	February	39
3	March	67
4	April	98
5	May	128
6	June	159
7	July	189
8	August	220
9	September	251
10	October	281
11	November	312
12	December	342

January 1st

I used to write memoirs in the form of pensive dreams from fabrication

A stark mutilation of firing neutrons in defense of cursive thoughts impeding

Id lead to the point of being lead
  Feeding said memories a deficit of love
    Oh.. how I used too

I used to wage wars with no casualties at face value
Unloaded of burden,
  Burnt & peeling,
   Asking for mercy,
    Oh.. how I used too

-January 2017 Dodge Corrections Chronicles

Everyone is at war with themselves in some fashion, and the results are rarely visible to our neighbor. What used to be isn't anymore.

January 2nd

The snows crawling & the list goes on
The wind's whispering sins of the summers fall
I called again just to hear your voice,
 If heavens just a step away,

 I hope your *close*

It's cold come morning so watch your soul
 Ice often covers the heart of the bold
I might just leave, go and hunt the heat,
 And leave these memories at sullen feet

-January 2020 another frigid lakeshore winter

I think sometimes the people we feel the most distant from are still the closest to our souls.

January 3rd

Sometimes I wear pants that don't fit,
 Just to step in discomfort,
& when my shoes seem to quit,
 I mutter sweet nothings to cover,
  My own thoughts,
   'til I only hear my soles (*soul*)
      Meet the rocks

-January 3rd 2023 a warm winter night

I always miss the point of doing something new. I forget the reason and worry about the results.

January 4th

I flounder out to sea until salt meets my wounds,
A familiar pain that never changes,
 Almost vital to survival
Below deck scraps,
Between logic & reason,
 Draw a crowd in my head
Men waste away fighting a battle blind to their neighbor,
 But painted to the world,
  Pull the cord on faith,
   Face the love left at the door

-Sept. 2014 writings from rehab

I wrote this in September but it feels like January. In the middle of some snow storm, out on some sea I'd never sail.

January 5th

I see the past in your eyes,
  The *joy*,
    The *pain*,
      The *hops*
        & the *rye*
Missile guided mistakes to the front lines of time
Marinate inside the locked cells of your soul as you cry
I'm the plaintiff of this plot,
  The antagonist to some
   And when the last chapters turned,
    The hero to none
Run, Run, boy you won't get far,
Flying blind with your head to the stars

-January 2021 drunken scribbles

I think I wrote this like a song.

January 6th

The bright lights of the city
always stare back at me,
  Maybe I ditched reality again,
   These fallacies we follow are
laughable
   Maybe I'm back again,
The hollow trees echo feeble
screams
 Of years of tattered
memories,
  The windows crisp with the
coming cold
    They're just moldy hearts,
     We've turned to gold

-January 2014 a date I can't remember

The result of a long walk to score.

January 7th

The bridges all burn across my battle torn mind,
I find signs of broken promises scattered about the frontlines
Time is relative until it's not,
  We bank on the unknown,
   What a twist in the plot,
Scars from our past always lay up together
 As we sit in the fence of a midnight bender,
We fend for our lives under whiskey on ice,
 Lying with the cover of neon lights

-January 2014 a walk with my regret

Sometimes I would burn bridges and use that as an excuse to continue the actions that would burn more.

January 8th

I hear the walls closing in,
 The door *latch*,
  My mind follows
I swear it will be different
 However many years I lie here,
  Is *enough*
Tough personas guarding broken hearts,
Muffled cries of regret,
 For love forgotten

-Jan. 2017 a prison cell in Wisconsin

This is one of those poems that I remember everything about, the sounds, the smells, my thoughts.

January 9th

I'm dust in the wind,
 Blown away by a song,
  Humming melody's,
   My feet meet the ground
I think I'm just another
mommas boy,
 Fooled by lungs full of smoke

-January 2022 it just fits

Are Januaries as historically bad for you as they are for me? I notice patterns like these and the food for thought I'm always left with is; maybe I'm predisposing myself to have a bad month because it's all I've known.

January 10th

The windows cry tears from the soul
 & sometimes eyes,
  Stare through the heart of the world
The winters cold,
 But we're used to this ,
  Another kiss in the wind,
   A gust of sin,
    I pray we don't float amiss

-Jan. 2017 the dungeon of Dodge Correctional

Sometimes, I'd pretend that the condensation that would build those cold mornings, were the tears I wasn't able to let out.

January 11th

Don't believe everything you think,
 You might sink,
& the captain doesn't have to go down with the ship
The birds sing before spring,
 To remind winter it's mortality
  It just so happens we need the same

-Jan. 2022 a robin appears in the snow

There is no honor in forgoing change for the sake of honoring the loyalty to one's self.

January 12th

I'm chasing sanity in
darkness,
 Losing touch with each step,
  I'm reaching out in silence,
   Searching for the sound of
my breath
They say it's always this calm,
 In the eye of the storm,
  But I feel the thunder,
   & the wind *shakes* my core

-a random scribble on a random page

I think everyone's eye of the storm looks a little different.

January 13th

Tree's after Christmas,
 Never look the same
  & April does nothing,
   But turn snow to rain
Is the world chasing fame?
 Or just the money behind it,
Sometimes a puzzle isn't done,
 Even if you solve it

-January 2022 it's time to take the tree down

Or leave it up, the logic is interchangeable,

January 14th

I feel like there is a muzzle to my head,
 & I'm barking like a dog,
  But no one can hear me,
   As my lungs start to fog,
Instead I bow to the crowd,
 & exit stage left,
  Off to my corner to write,
   A round of applause in my head

-January 14th 2023 today I'm my own applause

I'll be my own applause if I have to.

January 15th

Tears keep falling from the
sky,
 I see red eyes in the
distance,
Out of control I cruise,
 Desperate for the distance,
We finish from the start,
 You must of missed it

-January 15th 2023 on a rainy drive home

My biggest failsafe for my mental health is when I notice myself getting desperate for distance.

January 16th

I miss you on days like these,
 You'd roll over,
  With those puppy dog eyes,
   & ask me not to leave,

& I *wouldn't*

Because *nothing* was as important
 As the memories I now keep,
  Under lock & key

-January 2022 a fool lucky to love

Cherish love, no matter the form, and give it freely, regardless how cliche it sounds.

January 17th

Life isn't fair,
 But sometimes,
  Despair is chosen
Crowned by a king of it's own
exposure,
Forever has a line,
 A finite that can't be crossed,
  But if you wander off course,
   I won't call you lost

-January 2015 Outagamie County Jail Kitchen

I had to learn not to settle with myself.

January 18th

We all lack love in a changing world,
 Cold shoulders from old souls,
  Boldly take centerfold,
& I'm *tired*,
 On the edge of exhaustion,
  Holding perseverance hostage

-January 2022 a gentle reminder

The world doesn't make sense but it's my responsibility to take care of this little corner of reality I shape.

January 19th

I keep stumbling upon lodging,
 Vacant of sense,
  My heads homeless,
   Loaded off pipe dreams,
    Distorted with focus

-January 2017 the barracks of Dodge Correctional

I can only trip into tragedy so many times before I pinpoint the prominence of the position I play.

January 20th

Too often,
　I pretend I am this character,
　　In a plot I wrote,
　　　For only me,
& whenever the credits roll,
　I just want you to know,
　　You're the antagonist I
defeat

-January 2022 my favorite script

I miss the old DVDs, with different Menus to choose from; deleted scenes, alternate endings, the good ol days seemed so much better.

January 21st

I wish my mind worked like
back then,
 Before the *love*,
  The *smoke*,
   The *rush*,
    & the *gin*,
Before the lights went out,
 On a reason for fear,
  & the life I chased,
     Saved face in the mirror

-January 21 2023 another

corny wish

If my mind worked like back
then I wouldn't be writing this
no

January 22nd

I remember,
 When the shades weren't drawn,
   When dawn came quick,
    & the days too long
The weight of it lies,
 On light of the soul,
   Always grasping for warmth,
    But meeting just cold

-January 2022 & that day I didn't let the sun in

At one point I went from being so anxious to get out of work and back to the little life I created to staying at work to avoid it.

January 23rd

I feel like falling off a cliff,
　Just for a different point of view,
I still remember her lips,
　If I didn't it'd feel rude
　　I'm running with new laces
　　　But the faces all remain
　　　　If it's just a taste then waste it,
I'm searching deserts for my name

-January 2014 a fugitive from Arizona

I always thought I could just run away, physically and mentally.

January 24th

Ah,
 What a bittersweet treasure,
  To dig up the loot but bury forever,
It was supposed to be two,
 Locking arms on deck,
  Moving as one through violin steps

-Jan. 2017 the Dodge Correctional library

Life always balances out when buried treasure is involved.

January 25th

A *moment* of madness,
A *moment* of forever,
 Polaroid captures of
beginnings of never,
 If God let me choose,
  A new life at the end,
I'd raise a toast to hindsight,
 Finding my heart again

-January 2022 coping with

moments

Moments make up everything.

January 26th

Cobblestone roads born from dirty hands,
 Callus bear feet,
  The miles traveled,
   Wear & tear on the heartstrings,
Pain brings change,
 Love does too,
& the loss of both is sung,
 Through dive bar fools

-January 2022 I wish bar stools could talk

Don't forget that love can bring just as much positive change as pain does.

January 27th

Because I wander too,
 Through my emotions at night,
  Fighting demons who were once,
   Angels on the dark side of my mind,
I found extra time,
 In some corner I can't describe,
  But I know the feelings real,
   It's how I feel alive

-January 2017 Dodge Correctional chronicles

"When I notice someone else is stuck up at night, it reminds me I'm not alone in these cells" some guy in my cell

January 28th

I wish you could see the water through my eyes,
 Blue ice rises to meet the sun,
  Shimmering light reflects,
  Off untamed waves,
    As love caves in,
      The current gives way

-January 2014 the nastiest motel in FL

No matter what, I always take into consideration that waves are different heights, to different people.

January 29th

Just a sitting duck,
 With writer's block,
  Watching the clock hands chase,
   Something they're not
The sunset in Sedona,
 Tells a story of its own,
& the snow back home,
 Tastes a smudge like southern soul

-January 29th 2023 a patio in Tucson

I've learned it's impossible to not feel homesick, after you've left a little bit of your heart in different places and people.

January 30th

& then I'll fool myself,
 Into another last round,
  It's either I or myself,
   Who's in trouble tonight,
I'm just gonna follow the clouds,
 I might catch the sky,
  It's just the man and the moment,
    He watches life pass him by

-January 2014 a drunk night in Boynton Beach

The thing I'm most curious about, is when I approach the end, what are the moments I'm going to watch stride by.

January 31st

Shoes hit the beaten path unscathed,
  But come back battered,
   Worn to the *sole* of the *soul,*
As roots meet skin callused
 My hands brush the trees,
  My knees tickle leaves,
   My faith tested,
    On a breath,
     That the trail gets wider
As with life,
 We find space brings comfort,
  That's why I search for open roads

-Jan 31st 2023 some patio in Tucson

It's important to let myself trust

February 1st

It seems I've been wanderin'
all the places
 I've always been,
  With some sins in my
pocket,
   That never seem to last,
I got a one-way west,
 Just searching for the sun,
  Came back with lungs filled
with dust,
   But my head held high
These canyons echo the
memories of stone,
 Miles too long for the mind to
hold
So I'll tow my hope through
these cavern walls
 It's either me or myself or no
one at all

-that same patio in Tucson

I've never gone on a hike and
not been able to write a poem
after.

February 2nd

I wish I knew where to start
How do you carve love out of
stoned hearts?
I sit in the back trying to
outrun my past
 On the last mile when I
buckle,
  Another collapse
A pattern of disaster would
you look at me now
Loving what matters
 & reaching for clouds
Turns out I frown when I smile
 & I don't know how
Missing out on a life I was
trying to build in denial

-February 2014 a greyhound station in Orlando

I spent a long time chasing love in all different forms, natural and artificial.

February 3rd

I'm living for the fade away as the clock winds down
 And I'm *smoking* all my sins away,
  For a night on the town
I'll follow the orange till I suffocate it's glow
It's as simple as love,
 But we can't let the hate go
I'm late to my own funeral,
 I guess I'm fixing fate
  Chasing dates in a calendar,
   I never seem to make
Another sucker with a number,
 I'm just waiting in line
  Saving time on a watch,
   I never seem to find

-February 2014 an alleyway in Mobile, Alabama

Alleyways are usually more scared of you than you are of them.

February 4th

Crafted murals lead our way
 Tools for fools to lose their reason on
The breeze is cool under the deserts weight
 Another night I'll leave the light on
I banter with fate in broken tongues
 Trying to save face with sold out lungs
  This tale of the tape paints a bitter end
   As I show up to the gates with diminished funds

-February 4th a suite in Las Vegas

I've been trying to translate signs from fate for as long as I can remember and I don't know if I've ever scribed correctly.

February 5th

The tick of the clock,
 Ties my stomach in knots,
  Mortality breathes where
fear has not,
Leave the light on upstairs,
 So I make it out alive,
  I've been fighting my eyes,
   For a chance at life,
& never in my mind did I worry
I'd fall,
 There was peace with the
drop,
  From the top of it all,
Speed dial calls to a number
disconnected,
 Reminds me why,
  I keep this place so empty

-February 2017 Dodge Correctional Chronicles

When I finally got to prison, I got a light switch.

February 6th

The poems I wrote before,
 Don't matter now,
  How ironic
Almost like the wind,
 Of yesterday,
  Is forgotten
But over time,
 Even the strongest of stone,
  Withers away

-February 6th 2023 a lasting Wisconsin winter

This is one of my favorites.

February 7th

Dusk brings light
 Covered with dust
  A sight of disgust
   To my lonely mind
As dawn draws near
 The street signs sigh

Another late night
Another goodbye

-February 7th 2023 the street sign outside my house

There was this street sign outside my parents' old house and every time it snowed, the 19th century street lamp that bridged the median would catch the sign perfectly.

February 8th

Today I took the scenic route,
 All the way home,
  Past the echos from meadows,
   That sneak to the road,
I found peace all alone,
 Now there's not many left
Which was really the goal,
 When I noticed the mess
  That makes up these fools,
   Drowning in pools of our youth,
Stuck on stools by the fire avoiding snow in recluse

-February 2023 some 32,000 ft in the air

Always take the scenic route if you get the chance, you never know what adventure awaits.

February 9th

Oh how the wind speaks,
 In foreign whispers,
  From fallen kings,
The same words,
 As those they slew,
  Rang out,
If you listen close,
 You can hear the earth
repeat,
  Over and over

-February 9th 2023 I watched Lord of the Rings

It's important for me to be aware of my own history so I don't pass on my mistakes.

February 10th

The city seems to shudder,
 When the moon finally breathes,
The street signs dance with spotlights,
 At the mercy of the breeze,
I wish I could encompass,
 What this nighttime finally frees,
  But if I did-we'd greet the sun,
& I have date set with my dreams

-February 2014 snow in Memphis?

Snow has such a different texture and complexity when high that nullifies the beauty sober.

February 11th

I live in regret,
 In memories I wish I'd forget,
  But they're cherished
I bear burdens

I *shouldn't*,
 But I *couldn't*,
  When I *should* of,

Now I dance with what if's,
 My sanity on the fence,
  I just wish it'd come home

-February 2017 Dodge Correctional Chronicles
Shoulda, coulda, woulda, all of the above, these are the biggest burdens I sit with.

February 12th

I'm sitting with my toes in the ocean,
 Nestled into the sand,
  That's absorbing all the *moisture*,
   I won't let out of my head

-February 2014 scolding winter, missing the ocean

One of my favorite things about the Ocean is how vast it looks, truly incomprehensible.

February 13th

The snow falls again
 Can you *hear* it?
  Circling the wind
   Whispering sins
So here I stand
 In the middle of the end
  Just to hear it again
   Once & for all

-February 13th 2023 shoveling snow off a balcony

Not everything needs an explanation.

February 14th

I broke *you*
 You broke me
I saved I
 You saved **we,**
So many years,
 So many lives
Unwind each memory we lost
in the vines
 Grapes for your buzz
  Juniper for mine
   A *boy* drunk off mortality
    A *girl* crying over time
It's the fairy tale without the ending
 A random act without the kind

-February 14th 2023 a v-day reflection

Just here to remind you even if you've been through the ringer, it's still important to keep your heart open. Human connection is a gift.

February 15th

The path to nowhere begins right here,
 With 2 fingers of pine under ice
The real action starts,
  When the lights fade out,
    & when the games on the line,
     Luck doesn't count
I'll fall out,
 Before I lean into love
  Drunk off fumes,
   Were not meant to ingest
I'll suggest the ending before I read the script
& panic when the plot doesn't make sense

-February 2020 probably drunk

Don't be "that person" who only reads the last chapter & presents a book report on it the next day.

February 16th

Fools gold,
 In every sense of the phrase,
  Heavy bear those arms of burden,
Just curdled wholesome words welcomed,
 Among thieves In a crowded den,
We're isolated from a connection of worth,
 Lured to a throne of loud noise,
  Engulfing the only voice of value,
   The only voice with reason

-February 2022 sometimes were wrong

It was humbling for me when I finally accepted that I wasn't the person I had drawn up in my head. I remember specific emotions of guilt when writing this.

February 17th

I wonder if you wonder like me,
 On this side of forever,
  Speaking nevers to new lovers,

Drifting aimlessly

I'm just faithfully pacing,
 Across the same old trail,
  Failing to see beauty,
Where it once was before

-February 2022 4am work truck naps

Hindsight has the unique ability to alter memories and in doing that alter the emotions attached to my memories.

February 18th

I fly close to heaven,
 As I run from myself,
 Ironically tragic when you have nothing left,
A mess of a man who wanders alone,
 Chasing philosophy as though,
  It might make sense of his woes,
Love always atones for the hate now adjourned,
 The verdict is sudden,
  The jury's been torn,
The roof needs repairs,
 & the basement is flooded
I'll just sit in the kitchen,
 Where the fire first started

-February 2017 Dodge Correctional chronicles

Philosophy did, in fact, make sense of my woes.

February 19th

The clouds look different
 Like they've closed distance
today
Maybe it's a swing
 & a miss
  At forgiveness,
   Maybe they're astray,
The moon ends with dawn,
 Anticipating dusk,
  What a rush to exist,
   Among colors so lush

-February 2022 I wish clouds could talk

My favorite part about the transition from Winter to Spring is the shift in my perspective that for some reason allows me to appreciate the clouds more.

February 20th

These *gray* mornings,
 Plant *gray* thoughts,
 But even grief will bloom,
My mind soothes,
 In defense,
  A restless caustic,
   At best,
    Chasing purpose,
     Out of breath,

Trying to rhyme my way *home*

-February 2017 Dodge Correctional chronicles

One of my favorite quotes is "Your joy is sorrow unmasked".

February 21st

So I *clench*,
 & you *grasp*
& we're moved to such a degree,
 That I flee at first instinct
  Sinking beneath myself,
   Please tell the souls what sold them

-February 2022 trying to keep it all intact you know

One day I didn't have to run anymore & if I could bottle that process up and give it away I would.

February 22nd

Silent sounds fill the air between us,
  Can you hear it?
I find I lean on fear to remind myself of reason,
The snows been piercing,
  Under the grayest of skies,
    Like a warning from above,
      To capture the sun on the rise

-February 2022 winter has to end eventually

When the quiet starts to become noise I usually lose poise

February 23rd

The Melodies we seek,
 Are often hiding underneath,
  A labyrinth of keys,
   Only were allowed to see

-February 2017 Dodge
Correctional chronicles

I can't expect the world to be in tune when I keep all the notes hidden.

February 24th

I *miss* the rain on the stained glass,
 Movie scene tears wash away,
  The guilt of a person I never got to know
I *miss* the last pass I never finished
 A silhouette winner sits,
  Waiting for applause to gauze his mind
I *miss* the consistent
 The time-lapse of signs,
  On repeat through my eyes

-*February 2020 drunken scribbles*

My favorite recurring general scene you'll see in movies is when the camera catches the rain striking the stained glass window of a church.

February 25th

What a pleasant mistake,
 To drift away from this idle life,
  & into tomorrow blind,
But the sighs from the crowd,
 Speak over the laughter,
  So I'm stuck saving face,
   For a happily ever after

-February 2014 someone's couch in Wisconsin

Life was always more interesting for me when I had no idea what was going to happen tomorrow.

February 26th

The moon stayed up to greet me
 I find comfort in that fallacy
Quiet trees speak stoic ironies
 & those words they used to haunt me
It feels like my times up
 & just beginning
  It's getting hard to relay
   But I guess that's fitting

   Since I'm wandering astray

-February 2022 3:30am wake up

My most productive day's begin with a good night to the moon and a good morning to the sun

February 27th

I feel the calm in the air,
 I pretend you do too,
  I hate this time of year,
   I know you do too
But we're fools in the summer,
 It's good to recluse,
  & see through the gray,
   What were willing to lose

-February 2022 I wrote a lot in '22

Winters in Wisconsin start to feel so long by the time the end of February comes along.

February 28th

I wanna get away,
 But the still of the snow is sedating,
So I leave fate waiting,
 Like a romantic at dusk,
I forgot the fuss I made over love,
 How ironic

-February 2014 Dodge
Correctional chronicles

I try to remember life is a cycle and apply that when applicable.

March 1st

I don't know if God's real,
  But I've seen glimpses of *proof*,
    & I don't know life's truth,
    But I've seen glimpses in *you*,
These roots dig deep,
  Well beneath the garden,
  Hardened by horrors,
  Of the vast lost below the bottom

-March 2022 trying to trust the process

As soon as March hits it feels like it should be Spring to me. I wish I made the rules.

March 2nd

I adjust my rear view mirror,
 To compliment the cracks,
  Elastic hearts snap in the
face of value,
Tattered sheets,
 Meet the silk underneath,
  Playing peace in a melody,
Soothing to *you*,
& perfect to *me*

-March 2016 separated by jail doors

I have the ability (or curse) to modify reality to suit my needs. I am well trained in this art.

<u>*March 3rd*</u>

I tend to overstep my tendencies,
 In a feeble attempt at surrendering,
  To my own complacency,
   That I never let you see
Midnight leaps through my mental canvas,
Just to paint a picture of my epitome,
 That hasn't come to be

<u>*-March 2020 a random note to my subconscious*</u>

Pretty much been consistently at battle with myself for a hot minute. There have been phases where it's been better and worse, I was always convinced that only I had this phenomenon. Come to find out the whole world does.

March 4th

I'm here for another lonely night,
 Under sparks of light & smokey air,
  Bear my burdens,
   Until the season turns over ,
    It's cold outside,
     & my minds begun to wear,
But I'll fight beyond reason,
 I lose all logic on you

-March 2020 something about a pandemic

My favorite patio in the whole world is one that's full of smoke & I'm no smoker. It reminds me that people can make a place home.

March 5th

Elusive souls,
 Of old but young
  Speak in foreign,
   Broken tongues
Of memories,
 & blurry visions
  Of love,
   Of change,
    & indecision
In the back,
 My sleeves dyed red,
  Oh how my heart,
   Hopes this never ends

-March 2021 people watching at a bar

I could have written this about prison and it would fit just as well as a bar.

March 6th

I think times running out,
 My watch is full of scramblin' hands,
  Tan from a sun I never see,
   I walk with wonder till it's real,
I think my minds runnin' wild,
 In a maze of denial,
  I'm just filing away love,
   For my demise I never scheduled

-March 2022 sober notes

When I first started to get out of my degeneracy in my late 20s it always felt like I was behind.

March 7th

Sometimes I forget what it's like,
 To be so close to death,
  Yet finally feel alive
   Betting on silence,
    The heavy favorite
Another underdog story ends in statistics
I miss it,
 Not the rush,
  But the story
I know It's corny,
 A veteran of my own demise,
  Seeking out subtle sorries

-March 2017 Dodge Correctional chronicles

I've always used poetry as a way to cope, yet I've always felt embarrassed by the response it elicits when I cry or show outward emotion.

March 8th

There's got to be more,
 To these early mornings
  Than 5 min naps,
   & coffee black,
I'm trying to make a way,
 In what I thought was a warm world,
  Now shivering cold in the sun,
   Watching all I love grow old

-March 2022 jobsite notes

Sometimes I need to remind myself that I have to enjoy life. It's too easy for me to get caught up in everything I think I have to do.

March 9th

I'm alone getting high,
 Under chandeliers &
diamonds,
  How enlightening,
What an ironic way to fade,
 Why do I prefer the gravel,
  To the paved roads
   I've made my bed in,
How close I must of came

-March 2016 some trap house in Milwaukee

For a long time chaos reigned supreme over calm for me. I was comfortable in that.

March 10th

I bathe in the spring,
 Anticipating summer,
There's love lost in the corner,
 The oak trees couldn't cover,
But sometimes on my stroll home,
 I see a flower bloom,

She *loves* me,
She *loves* me not

-March 2017 Dodge Correctional chronicles

Flowers are the most beautiful when you least expect to see them I think.

March 11th

When does the wind,
 Become the melody,
  Keeping secrets safe,
   From seeing ears,
I yearn for freedom,
 But doubt the free,
  Another defensive wound to heal,
Save my last meal for breakfast
 I won't miss my alarm,
  & if I do I'll find my stool,
   Among a dive bar in the clouds

-March 2020 a drunken melody

I learn something new from someone every day.

March 12th

I quit waiting for the sun,
  The beauty was intoxicating,
   Maybe if I wake up to the dark,
    It won't be as suffocating,
The world is suffering,
The slowest demise,
 But time is relevant,
  Too peace of mind

-March 2017 Dodge Correctional chronicles

A warning sign for me and my mental health is if I start waking up on either end of the sun not being out. I'm either waking up way too early or taking late night naps upsetting my circadian rhythm.

March 13th

Souls need saving,
 Before faces,
  But there's a deficit of love
on the horizon,
Eyes hide behind the fog,
 With just the wind,
  & the calm
Fighting yesterday's
tomorrow,
 At the cost of it all

-March 2022 finally feeling like me again

Tomorrow, can quite literally, steal today and I've noticed it can happen in an instant, right when I'm feeling like me again.

March 14th

I paint prophecy's in the white,
 That no one will ever read,
  It's quite quiet out here,
  But I can't hear myself breathe,
This is destiny written,
 I'm just forbidden to know,
  How to suppress the shiver,
   When you fold on your soul

-March 2022 one of those mid-march snowstorms

Clothes can always be unfolded and reorganized. I think the soul works the same.

March 15th

I'm stuck conforming to
distorted minds
 I pass the right for the left
  I don't think I'll ever decide
I'm back on the side,
 Of a road you'll never find,
  With my thumb up high,
   Whistlin' nothings to no one,

It's so *sweet* in my mind

-March 2017 Dodge Correctional chronicles

I always strive to put myself in a position where I'll never have to feel stuck in a place that's not comfortable to me again unless I choose.

March 16th

If we met again for the first time,

Would you cry?

Knowing what you know now about life,
 How would you love twice?
  Knowing how the movie ends

-March 2016 a drug induced love

How different it is watching a movie for the second time.

March 17th

I'll probably never see all of
you,
 At least,
Not in the way,
I
Want to,
I
Want to see you like the
clouds,
 Happy,
  Angry,
   Light,
    & *dark*,
But not all wonders are meant
to be discovered

-March 2020 drunken scribbles

& if I'm lucky enough to see
every wonder I've imagined,
I'll never be short of stories in
the end.

March 18th

I'm secreting a creation,
 Like an infant with some crayons,
& sometimes the deepest art,
 Are just scribbles of the wind,
  Ironically its blowing,
   My hair across my eyes,
    So even if I wanted,
The meaning couldn't find my sight

-March 2022 mischievous art

The joy on a child's face seeing their art displayed on the fridge.

March 19th

I'm writing poems about a
love,
 That never really existed,
  Like a memory,
   That becomes saturated,
    With lie after lie,
     Until the movie on repeat,
      Radiates perfection

-March 2015 Brown County Jail diaries

I really am capable of writing, directing and critiquing a whole movie in my head.

March 20th

One day you whispered,
 Life is fate
  & fate is freedom
  & that concept always
leaves me,
   A step past seething,
Because it doesn't make any
fucking sense,
 Until it does

-March 2022 post-therapy
notes

I firmly believe that life is a cycle and having free will inside a circle gives me comfort.

March 21st

Sometimes I miss the blanket,
 My inner child *gripped*,
Wrapped in a deficit of love
 I never realized I *missed*
& sometimes I get timid,
 Replaying scenes I deleted
  Wrapped in memories I *depleted*,
   From an already leaking brain

-a broken spoken word

I didn't realize how things that happened in my childhood shaped the human I became until I was able to be honest enough with myself about what I needed.

March 22nd

Before the rain there's a scent,
  Like a bulb before a bloom,
   Waiting in unison with us,
    For some higher approval,
     Like a gunshot,
      Shock starting a race

-March 2022 50/50 rain or snow

There is no better scent to come back to now with than that of an impending rain.

March 23rd

I realize I've tested each memory,
 To see which I should remember first,
  As if it should be the best one,
But that would minimize life's experience,
 To the extent of my head

-March 2017 Dodge Correctional chronicles

Big therapy advocate, I think everyone should experience that beauty in their life.

March 24th

Sometimes,
 I feel like the quarters on the floor,
  The ones you walk right by,
   As if they were dimes,
No,
 Pennies,
  I'm that detached from your reality,
   Just a copper memory,
    In the cracks of a society you built,
Just for you

-March 2022 when the fog starts to lift

I collect all change so I had to go outside my own perspective.

March 25th

I'm acting on the notion,
  That I'm better off alone
Like a bird avoiding winter,
  My soul rides the wind home
But the nest no longer exists,
  All the trees uprooted
   If it's true ignorance is bliss,
    Then the truth must be
euphoric

-March 2014 should of stayed in Florida

If, like me, you learn by trial & error, please pay close attention to the results. Abide by the logical deduction done outside of your control.

March 26th

& before you go,
 Turn off the light,
  I prefer to suffocate on memories,
   In the darkest of silence

-*March 2017 Dodge Correctional chronicles*

It's important for me to process things in silence, it helps me not be influenced by outside variables.

March 27th

& one day Wisdom
whispered,
 In a tongue I can only
describe,
　As the very moment lungs
greet cords,
　　The moment instinct
decides to survive
"Tomorrow isn't real"

-March 2022 the tables

sometimes turn

If your imaginary friend is
wisdom then I promise you're
on the right track (I think).

March 28th

I use poetry,
 As therapy,
& although it's seems to save me,
Some days,
 I miss the fog,
  Of a battle,
   I don't even *remember*

-March 2022 post-therapy notes

I've never not written a poem after therapy.

March 29th

I'm preemptively leaving,
 My mind exits stage left,
  In an attempt to drown
 Out the applause
  With all the boo's I still dread

-March 2016 false praise breeds destruction

I'm my own worst critic, sometimes I'm too hard on myself and sometimes not hard enough.

March 30th

I still say your name,
 Even though you're not around,
 The same way I mutter God's,
  As though this time around,
   I might hear a response

-March 2017 Dodge Correctional chronicles

Whoever I'm choppin' it up with upstairs is definitely responding, it just took me much longer to translate than it should have.

March 31st

Sometimes I loathe the
fundamentals,
 The commas,
  The *emphasis*,
   The spacing of sentences,
Sometimes I just beg,
 Whoever's reading,
  To find their message

-March 31st 2023

As I started compiling this collection, I began to get more critical in my writing style. I felt like I had to learn to write like a published poet to be a published poet.

April 1st

I play my hand with reckless hope
 Confused,
  How I was even awarded,
  A seat at this table
The deck is stacked
 My mind is torn,
But I love the rush against the odds

-April 2016 drug induced diaries

I feel like I'm in certain places at certain times for a reason and even if this is completely in my head, it manifests in real life thoughts and decisions

April 2nd

I feel I'm something of a cynic,
 Who somewhere along the way,
  Received such love,
   That dead flowers didn't matter,
    I could fixate on the bloom,
     Even if they're few

-April 2022 post-therapy notes

Therapy with someone who is willing to point out your biases and prejudices to help me see things rationally, not just based on my experience alone, was key for me.

April 3rd

I'm trying to find a motive,
 To use motion,
  To satisfy some longing,
   That *maybe*,
    Just *maybe*,
Like a sailor lost at sea,
 In the eye of the perfect storm
  Riding the calm amongst the sunset,
   Convinced that,
    Everything might actually,
Be *okay*

-April 2017 Chippewa Correctional thoughts

There's something to be said that a lot of people find comfort in the idea of being lost.

April 4th

& one day I started running,
  Like this guy Forrest,
   In this movie I grew up on
& I couldn't stop,
  With each staggered breath,
   & each stumbled step,
I got a bit closer to my mind

-April 2022 it was like 2010 all over again

I love running, I don't know what it is but I just go into another world, where there is nothing but calm.

<u>April 5th</u>

I think this path leads nowhere,
 & I think that's what I need
  Sometimes the point of failure,
   Points to the breath we won't release,
I'm leaving behind my mind,
 If I stop thinking I might see,
  The line I drew in the sand I turned,
   Burned the time I used to believe

<u>-April 2022 the next right thing</u>

I have never been led astray by doing the next right thing.

April 6th

Easter clouds tuck the moon
in,
 & I'll be the first to see,
  Memories through melodies,
   I feel we're painted just for
me,
The sun extorts its canvas,
 A sacrifice for scenery,
  The bandit of skies,
   I never knew I'd need

-April 2022 seeing the sky different

Sometimes I like to pretend
that the sky paints the sunsets
for me personally, I know this
is selfish but it feels good
nonetheless,

April 7th

I wish this had a happy ending,
 But wishes breed resentful results,
  Half of me is tempting,
   The other half to dissolve
Or resolved,
I can't hear through the fog,
Full of empty promises,
 I polished and set on the shelf

-April 7th 2022 I wonder if this is real

It's always been hard for me to detect if I'm living in my own truth. I spent so many years manipulating myself that it felt like everything was fabricated.

April 8th

Running out of gas on a one way,
 What a shame,
Burnin out on a Monday,
 Harassed by the rain,
These castles we chase,
 Are waiting to crumble,
On the backs of men,
 Who made deals with the devil

-April 2013 one of the first rehab poems I ever wrote

It feels to me like we're chasing the same castles we're waiting to fall on the men who own them now.

April 9th

The sun of spring,
 Brings the eve of summer,
  & the eyes of love meet their final slumber
I wait for the rise like a dog at the door
 It's beauty comprised with a ceiling for more
I tour my mind,
 & find such a waste
Just long lines,
 Without guidance,
  Trying to make their own way,
I fade out to a world where dreaming is king,
& float down with some lore I can't even explain

-April 2013 writings from rehab

April always felt like the transition from Spring to Summer for me.

April 10th

I wake up surrounded,
 By the light in the distance,
I don't miss the sun,
 Until the rain starts to kiss me,
I'm afraid of what's next,
 I can't see my steps,
So let's drink,
 & reflect,
  On the regret we just met,
Fates set in stone,
 We just decide how we get there,
& faith never folds,
 On a soul that's been squared

-April 2015 on the run with a bottle

It was so much easier to drink or drug away my problems in 2015 and I'm extremely grateful today that that notion has done a complete 180 turn.

April 11th

I *blink,*

& step *blind* off the ledge,

I hedge my bet with resent,
 I didn't know the risk,
  The reward never comes,
   When you gamble on love,
& the gin in my cup,
 Overflows to my lungs,
I gasp for air,
 I already know exists,
Not the fittest for survival,
 But I'm taking my licks

-April 2020 a covid alcoholic

Unhealthy defensive and coping mechanisms have always sprouted up in my life in very inconvenient ways.

April 12th

My soul steps in line,
 With the rise of your chest,
What a mess,
To be blessed with love,
 In a world filled with dread,
Credit to the courage,
 I never thought I'd find,
 To sit with myself,
  & finally feel alright

-April 2022 I see the light at the end of the tunnel

It took me a long time to realize how grateful I was for being capable of finding love, even when it doesn't last.

April 13th

I'll sift through the sand,
 & lose the soft of my hand,
& watch my ride find the
horizon,
 At the top of the land,
The sun meets my soul,
 As his brother brings the cold
Just my feet,
 & a hope,
  For something a little more

-April 2022 callused hands

Working 60-70 hour weeks through blazing hot summers & frigid winters taught me that hands aren't the only thing that loses softness.

April 14th

I've lost my train of thought,
 Along the route less traveled,
Let's have a toast to survival,
 Under the stars that still
shine,
  I'm climbing some mountain,
   In some corner of my mind,
    & everything feels rotten,
Like it's surrounded by sighs,

-April 2022 accepting the path

It was hard for me to accept that path that I was on, which was healthy & conducive to my goals, was the right path.

April 15th

When I lay down at night,
 I feel the rainfall inside,
The *pitter patter* on the roof,
 Sounds the same in my mind,
I line up single file,
 With me, myself & I,
& spy a light at the end,
 That's been waiting all night,
I tell the stars I'm heading home,
 Then I walk to the moon,
& talk to views,
 Under a shine,
 That so often soothes

-April 2013 I can never sleep

In a stark contrast to today, I used to stay up into the wee hours of the morning, unable to turn off my mind without some sort of substance.

April 16th

It's always okay to be here again,
 Adhered static strays dreary,
  Through my brain,
Same day deliveries,
 Of memories,
  In the cloudiest form,
Weathers the storm we know as time

-April 2022 it's okay to stumble backwards

I try to never use shame as a response to a lapse in flaws in my behavior. Snow still falls in April, even though winter ceases.

April 17th

Men seek value,
 Nothing less,
Stuffing pain in a bottle,
 Until they drink down the mess
The stars steer the way,
 To a sun up till the jobs done,
  Red in the face,
   From a strain that reaches,
   Deep,
    Down,
Dirty hands,
 & steel toe boots,
  Cigarettes,
   & joint stoned fools
Laugh & cry,
 Amongst the tune,
All the way home

-April 2022 a blue collar poem

A reminder to myself to never let a job affect my health.

April 18th

I'm on another path to nowhere,
 Stuck staring at the stars,
I'm facing fair tomorrow,
 Under the dimming light of now,
I'm screaming out in silence,
 This might all be in my head,
I used to chase the canvas,
 Until the colors bled,

-April 2022 I'm debating paths again

There have been many times on my journey where I've felt like I was on these paths to nowhere. There doesn't always have to be a destination.

April 19th

These chapters turn,
 & burn with the seasons,
Late night freedom,
 Leaves a lost man seething,
  His roads never swept,
 & his feet kick up dust,
Looking lust in the face,
 & pretending it's love

-April 2016 Outagamie County Jail scrawls

When I was locked alone with my thoughts I was forced to come to accept my own actions & dynamic.

April 20th

Sometimes a thumb high
sounds so appealing,
 Just highway ,
  & dirt,
Paint the details I'm fleeing,
I left the key to my heart,
 In empty bags by the road,
I plea with this art to smooth
the edge of my soul

-April 2013 the chance of a lifetime

If you ever get offered a
chance to move across the
country to chase health, I
suggest you take it,

April 21th

I drink from a glass,
  That never seems to empty,
& laugh with plenty,
  Who never understand me,
Now I stand on my own,
  Because I forgot how to lean,
Deleting scenes in this movie,
  I never thought I'd see,
Lead me to river,
  I'll follow it downstream,
   One day I'll reach the skyline,
    I do in my dreams

-April 2020 drunken scribbles

When I had all the free time in the world, my life was consumed by the glass.

April 22nd

I'm avoiding each breath,
 Like I have a choice in the matter,
  & I'm losing my voice,
   Like I ever spoke up when it mattered,
I'm mad I'm feeling mad again,
 I thought this phase might pass,
  Pushing saturated sadness,
  To fiends who never asked

-April 2022 these words help me realize

When I started taking poetry seriously again, I realized how often I stayed quiet instead of using my voice.

April 23rd

I can't hear myself think,
 Over the screech of
tomorrow,
 I'm borrowing time from a
watch,
  That hasn't ticked,
   Nor tocked,
    In forever,
If you blink,
 You might miss it,
But I'm not sure what it is,
 Tipping my hat to no one,
  Just to feel wholesome again

-April 2022 I want to hear my own thoughts again

I've noticed that if I stack too much food on my plate, I spend most of the meal thinking about how full I'm going to be tomorrow.

April 24th

I *wonder* if you *wander* like I
do,
 I hope you're not lost,
  Tossing' a thumb high,
   Up & down the coast,
I *wonder* if you *wonder* like I
do,
 Foolish dreams,
  Of priceless hours,
Subtle comfort of scenes,
 Known only to two,
I *wonder* about *love*,
 If it's real,
  If chasing the wind,
   Is worth this ordeal

-April 2022 too busy wonderin' & wanderin'

My imagination is only healthy if I don't take up residence there.

April 25th

Paint a picture with your
words,
  & leave me speechless,
   It's funny how we see fear,
    When we lose it,
It's easy on the eyes,
 When we believe all the lies,
 Just soothing my future
surely,
  With every last surmise

-April 2016 Outagamie County
Jail scrawls

There was a huge difference in my character when I lived with healthy courage, compared to when I lived with a lack of fear.

April 26th

Saddle up before the trail goes cold,
Another midnight ride,
In the search for gold,
Another rush,
Another fade,
Another 5 min of fame,
& when the dust settles,
We'll find it all the same
But here we are,
Lost in the stars,
Drunk off of pipe dreams,
We smoked with our scars,
My minds finally empty,
A welcomed surprise,
It seems the more pain I run from,
The more that I find

-April 2014 on the run with a bottle

Nothing changes if nothing changes.

April 27th

I've picked up the pen a
dozen times,
 But the fonts never right
  I capitalize the Y;
  In you I see my lies,
Now I crumble it up for
another

*-April 2017 Chippewa
Correctional thoughts*

My notebooks are filled with
failed love letters.

April 28th

I keep waking up to yesterday's sighs,
 Miles from my mind,
Rewinding scenes from my demise,
Time turns pale,
 As these poems on parchment,
Venting in cursive hurdles,
 Scribed in light across the darkness

-April 2013 writings from rehab

I've experienced waking up in one place physically but another mentally. Sometimes our mind goes on vacation without approved PTO.

April 29th

I'm breathing in the wind,
 & all its secrets,
Trying to find it's weakness,
 Hanging memories,
  From Leafless trees,
   Just hoping that you take them,
Save me from the sentiment,
 You leave in broken sentences,
I'm a miles away from a dream I faked,
Just to taste the lips I promised

-April 2022 writing scripts to movies, I've already seen

When I was a kid I'd pretend that storms would take with them the secrets I no longer felt I could hold onto. It gave me some fake sense of comfortability.

April 30th

I'll continue to weave phrases,
 Into a maze of worth,
I kiss the gaze you leave me,
 In place of dirt,
First always comes last,
 When you're cheating death,
  I scream into the glass,
Just to break at the neck

-April 2022 things don't always go right

Sometimes I can do the next right thing and still not get the desired results.

May 1st

Don't follow me,
 I leave a wake of cliches in my path,
  Made to soften,
   Fallen connections,
    Of love at first glance,
A chance taken for granted,
 Is taking the safe route for me,
  Chase away the responsibility,
   Of facing a better me,
Fate has a mind of its own,
 In this rented space,
Taped off with caution,
 As I slowly pace

-May 2022 simple living

Cliches are corny because they're more often than not true.

May 2nd

Another early morning,
Another restless night,
Weighted sounds of my past,
 Surround my head to fight,
Hands wrapped,
 To comfort the blows,
  But I feel each one connect,
Pain from hindsight grows,
 As it wraps its grip around my neck

-May 2013 writings from rehab

The more restless I spend the evenings, the more restless I spend the mornings.

May 3rd

This tomb feels too
comfortable,
 I thought I dug my way out,
  How sad to see my shadow,
  Finally followed me down,
It cowers for the hours,
 I fight off to cherish,
Embarrassed by the riot,
 It's attempting to manage,
I just fan off the smoke,
 It'll soon consume my lungs,
Full of *nothing*,
 It's never *enough*

-May 2013 writings from rehab

I always try to remember that I'm enough for myself or I wouldn't exist.

May 4th

My mind is a museum,
 My memories exhibits,
  & I exhibit selfish motives,
   When I start to reminisce,
I might finish where I started,
 & still call it a success,
  If the glass is already half empty,
   I may as well drink the rest,

-May 2022 remember my own history

I have yet to find the right formula that balances archiving history in a healthy manner and holding onto memories through attachment.

May 5th

I lace the pain I forget to hide,
 My lungs fill with *sighs screaming silent*,
A tyrant of my own design,
 It's ironic when quiet becomes violent,
  Eyes become vibrant,
   When the horizon shines dim,
Just two feet & some time spent,
 Waiting for when

-May 2016 Outagamie County Jail scrawls

Every human in this world laces their pain with something, everyone self-medicates.

May 6th

Face the music,
 If you can hum the tune,
  Lines fine as strings,
   Stroke chords that soothe,
Foolish views,
 Blind hindsights beauty,
  Surely feeling alone,
   Isn't always lonely

-May 2013 my intro to Arizona

In 2013 lonely was lonely, I was 18 halfway across the country with no idea what I was doing, no money to my name, just a bad dope habit.

May 7th

It seems like I'm runnin',
 I just don't know where,
My foot meets the puddle,
 Each step ripples with snare,
  I bare the weight of this
subtle accord ,
   I can't afford more pain,
    The deposits gone cold

-May 2022 post-run therapy

When I found the melody in my footsteps I found some silence in my head.

May 8th

I miss the grass between my toes,
 On road sides enclosed,
  Inside a younger me's imagination,
I'm facing constellations,
 Covered by the sun,
  Begging someone's someone,
   For patience,
Who never had one

-May 2022 a road trip

I used to get carsick as a kid, if I didn't have headphones on. Sometimes I wonder if it was my conscience wanting a break from the race to enjoy the present.

May 9th

It's different then,
  Just feet to pavement,
   I vs *me*,
    Intertwined seething,
With passion born of unclear motives
  Just hope for some stolen focus,
   Distraction from myself,
    Is a golden ticket,
     To my peace,
      Leased time,
       From whatever sign you cry for,
As you bow on your knees

-May 2013 running in the desert

I had to be present running at higher elevations, the body needs time to adjust, as with life.

May 10th

In my dreams,
 I'm sound awake,
  Through an afternoon snooze,
Cloudless skies gives us,
 A peak up to heaven,
  With a smile,
   & a nod to those gazing down,
Just a shallow loud of now to sit up with,
As gratitude fills my eyes,
 With thoughts now profound

-May 2013 newly sober dreams

The different dream phenomenon as the journey through sobriety and the different ways that looks was always so volatile.

May 11th

The door latches,
 As my mind unlocks,
  Pacing 8 by 6 feet in my dream,s
Slowly time flies,
 In the irony of routine,
Grasping onto love,
 In my head through deleted scenes,
Tentative thoughts,
 Breed a need for skewed perception,
To keep from,
 Losing human connection
Hate resonates,
 Through recycled air,
Bare,
 By the emotion,
  Of scars hidden,
   By the toughest glares

-May 2016 Outagamie County Jail scrawls

I always pace when I need to think, no matter how small the space, when my mind is running my body provides balance.

May 12th

I keep trying to dissect,
Each,

  Picture

   Perfect

    Moment

But I find I hold fear,
 Too dear to my heart,
  To open up the curtains
& let love in

—May 2022 changing societal norms

As a matter of fact it is completely normal for me to trust and let love in even though the status quo says I shouldn't.

May 13th

Mothers are strict,
 Like an asterisk,
  A fine print of love
Mom's are kind,
 The orange sky,
  Greets the night sky
Mama knows,
 The road I chose,
  Would always lead me,
   Back to love

-May 12th 2023 for mom

A Mothers Day for mom

May 14th

I find the proof in what's off putting,
 & politely recluse,
  To the same room I watched flood,
   With seconds to lose,
But it seems as far as I fall,
 The ending greets soft,
I'm just another hand on the clock

-May 2016 Chippewa Correctional thoughts

I've always been fortunate to get a relatively soft landing amongst the poor decisions that encompassed my 20s and I'm grateful for that.

May 15th

Pounding,
 Pounding,
  Blinding light,
Violent silence screams so bright,
A tyrant mind that was once my own,
Held captive by tones that once were warm

-May 2020 a slip into the bottle

I'm full of empty promises when I'm self-sabotaging, which is true irony.

May 16th

My lungs start to stutter,
 Just as the sun meets my gaze,
I mutter sweet nothings,
 As if that's something to praise,
I expect I'll forgo,
 The next compliment my way,
I'll save opening the door,
 For the day I know its safe

-May 2013 a foreign desert

A change in landscape from the midwest flat to the valleys and canyons of the desert is eye-opening, it forced a new perspective.

May 17th

It takes two to tango,
 & I'm dancing on my own,
  In the corner-faking sober,
  So I don't have to feel alone,
My phones always ringing,
 & I never wanna answer,
  Setting the standard low,
   So they can't blame me
later

-May 2020 creating a scapegoat

Through abusing substances & not treating mental health, I'm creating the perfect soil to grow a scapegoat to pursue the cycle of sabotage.

May 18th

I fold the corner over,
 I'm not ready for that chapter,
The protagonist burns,
 Over aesthetic laughter,
Do we end up lost?
 Comparing wounds we've gathered,
& what do we do,
 When the plot thickens,
 When tension shatters

-May 2022 picking up a book again

Somewhere along the way I realized reading is just as important as writing.

May 19th

Foul souls,
 Follow me home,
  I think they're after,
   The peace inside,
But I'm foolishly naive,
I've run the river dry

-May 2016 Outagamie County
Jail scrawls

I can't always escape the presence of others, but I can always control the access they have to me internally.

May 20th

Ah it's my own sign of the times.
  Toeing lines so fine,
   The lies forget to cry,
I see my breath,
 & I wish the warmth would follow,
   But I'll swallow my sorrow,
    & pass on dessert,
Looking for all the right reasons,
 In all the wrong hurt

-May 2022 does winter ever end?

When I start longing for summer in the midwestern Winters, I find myself paying acute attention to my breath and the visibility of it on my morning runs.

May 21st

I glance at my watch,
 & notice the race,
  Seconds chase minutes,
   I wish I could keep them at bay,
    Hours seem to pass,
     Without much to look back on,
      Until we're years in the past ,
       Regretting fears we fell deaf on

-May 2022 a run to remember

We live in a world where we critique ourselves but don't praise ourselves.

May 22nd

My footsteps used to fail me,
 But that's a tale for another day,
  The chaos seems so comforting,
   When the clouds paint your way,
The birds utter love,
 At the first taste of spring,
  Shivering in the sun,
   I wonder if the hummingbirds,
    Think we're dancing

-May 2022 a break in the clouds

It's always okay to recognize setbacks, they happen to me on a daily basis in some form.

May 23rd

My vision is blurry,
　mind erratic,
　　how ironic,
Self-destructive tendencies,
　Line my pockets again,
Another sin on the precipice,
　But we love to fall,
　　The sudden fear equals life,
　　　Until the curtain finally calls

-May 2015 the last day of a bender

I still live for the same exact thrill I chased when being actively addicted to drugs. I've learned to not set expectations on the dopamine I receive.

May 24th

I don't want to leave,
 But I have to go,
  I've searched low for a high,
   I couldn't ignore,
    I drained my account,
     Of every last breath,
Waiting for more from a world,
 Id never expect,
So I'll sit on the fence,
 With one foot out the door,
  Holding on to words,
   I've always adored

-May 2015 a poem to a girl who let me sleep on her couch

Keep an eye on your internal bank account.

May 25th

Often the peak of the fire,
 Is faceless,
I hope you save your voice for the day,
 You might use it,
I admire the lines I read the lies,
 In between,
It seems I'm stuck trying to escape,
 This teenage dream

-May 2022 Memorial Day approaches

It's been pounded into my head, for as long as I can remember, that peoples stories matter. I still refused to intentionally allow this notion into my life & it's so underrated.

May 26th

I took the backroads through
my past,
 I found the route scenic,
  A change from the horror,
   I used to hide in the smoke
with,
I sip from a glass,
 That used to shake in my
hand,
& taste the nostalgia,
 That calls to each man

-May 2021 just a normal drinker

For the longest time my biggest accomplishment was going from a Heroin addict to a normal drinker. I was so proud of being normal, just to find out it wasn't.

May 27th

Our youth isn't promised,
 But our truth is,
Foolish boys,
 Turn to men,
  Under moonlit skies,
Drunk off of hope for a restful night

-May 2013 writings from rehab

I wish I could bottle up my mindset from every time I've experienced a pink cloud and give it away as some sort of elixir.

May 28th

Words I form clear,
 Echo slurred to deaf ears,
  I fear the look the mirror gives,
   Isn't steered from my soul,
Bold to assume,
 I could carry the weight,
  It's safe to save face,
   Under the pretense of fate

-May 2022 the response is rarely what's expected

Not everything I say is going to be heard how I wanted it to. Not everything I do will be received how I wanted it to be.

May 29th

Cloudless skies,
 Gives me a peak up to heaven,
I imagine a smile,
 & a nod,
From those gazing down,
Just the soundless loud of now,
 To sit up with

-May 2022 traditions

Always have had a strong family connection to this day, remember our ancestors that paved the way for my family to continue prospering.

May 30th

Time stands with no one,
 We just chase after more,
Confined to somewhere,
 We've never been before
  The door stays locked,
   From the outside in,
    I'm at war with the clock,
     & there's no time left to win

-May 2016 Outagamie County Jail scrawls

I try to remember the clock is irrelevant, even though at the heart of my instinct it's the one thing I wish I could master.

May 31st

I'm just passively avoiding patience,
 In lieu of pensive thoughts,
& I'm up against oasis,
 In a never ending plot,
I'm a shot away from gorgeous,
 In tune with who I'm not,
 Mocking unknown forces,
  Praying to anything but God

-May 2014 writings from rehab

It's extremely difficult to feel the emotions correlated with addiction & feel close to spirituality at the same time.

June 1st

Sometimes,
 The pace seems *effortless*,
Heel to toe,
 Like a metronome,
Holding onto chopped
breaths,
 Rain meets sweat at the base
of my neck,
A steady thud,
 As I become distant from my
problems

-June 2022 running with some purpose

As I started to combine my love of poetry with the art of running, I noticed how seemingly unrelated things are really metaphors for each other.

June 2nd

I sold my reason for love,
 Under the southwestern sun,
I thought these souls,
 Could fold,
  Over scars
   We'd outrun,
But the seasons changing,
 The sunsets losing depth,
  The warmth is fading,
   I see through the smoke off
my breath

-June 2013 a desert full of lapses

Even 1,000 miles away from what I called home, I still found the same scars, renting space in the same place.

June 3rd

The street lights cry at sunset,
 As the moon sighs awake,
  Past the art of time,
I'm climbing mountains in my head again,
 & my souls falling behind,
  Maybe I'll find it at the sunrise,
   I've been chasing all night

-June 2022 the first sunset of summer

The biggest benefit I got from quitting drinking was having the peace of mind to be present during nature's favorite hours.

June 4th

I have a tendency,
 To articulate mistakes,
  That tempt fate,
I paid off my own soul,
 Just to watch it turn old,
  & get lost in the coldest way

-June 2020 drunken scribbles

I used to excuse my excess drinking habits by using the phrase, "At least I'm not using heroin". I was reminded not all problems are as dramatic as the worst case scenario. That doesn't mean they aren't serious within themselves.

June 5th

My breath is finally in recluse,
 Just a step towards summers eve,
Meet me where I'm at,
 But please don't leave me free,
  Keep the key under the stone.
   We both know where it lie,
Making up nothings
 But we can't fool our eyes

-June 2022 pleading through poetry

My adaptive way to journal now includes taking the feelings I would jot down and turning them into a picture of words.

June 6th

Silently speaking my mind to
no one,
  Or at least anyone of notice,
    I'm focused on my motives,
      My subconscious can be cut
throat,
I'll touch tomorrow with today,
  & recoil from the burn,
    I'm so far from yesterday,
I don't remember if it hurts

-June 2022 running into summer

As the seasonal depression starts to lift, I find it easier to dial in on my motives and the goals behind them.

<u>*June 7th*</u>

I keep tabs on lapses,
 That seep through my mind,
  Unwinding vines through my eyes,

I think I can finally *relax*,

I keep passing by the life,
 I always wished I had,
  & realize I'm lost in the palm of my hand

<u>-*June 2016 Outagamie County Jail Scrawls*</u>

If I could go back & tell the younger me who wrote this that he was <u>actually</u> in the palm of his hand & these weren't just clever words that sounded good next to each other.

June 8th

Sometimes,
 It seems the sun,
  Is falling from grace,
I'm bracing for the impact of a crash,
 I saw miles back,
It's like yesterday,
 Took tomorrow out,
  & shared all my secrets,
I just need a hero who isn't heroic

-June 2022 this feeling won't last

I tend to predict my demise before the goods even arrive. It's this cycle of trying to jump out in front of the negativity, that inevitably invites it over sooner

June 9th

I finally escaped comfort,
 By no skill of my own,
   I wonder if my chute will open,
    As I scramble back to earth,
Like a cat who slips out the back,
 & returns with a new reality,
  I'll strum my chords raw,
    But no one understands me

-June 2022 falling on deaf ears

It was really hard for me to convince people that significant changes I made were now boundaries. I'll forever cherish the people in my life who didn't miss a beat in supporting me.

June 10th

Love isn't *given*,
 At least not in the way,
  You hand a child a french fry,
   In the backseat,
    On the way home,
It's like a monsoon,
 Reigning terror,
  & providing life,
   In the same breath

-June 2013 rain in Northern Arizona

I'm always in awe of nature's wrath, from experiencing Tropical storms to Winter ones, tornados to monsoons, there is true beauty in the far off terror that isn't quite at your doorstep.

June 11th

There's a method to this madness,
 We've yet to uncover,
  It could be hanging from the rafters,
   Among cluttered antique treasures,
Or in alleyways,
 In brains,
  Muttering names,
   Of old lovers

-June 2022 uncovering the key to functional insanity

I've noticed that a lot of times, the most outlandish thing I try to resolve an issue, often works. The most difficult part is convincing myself to push past the delusion.

June 12th

I'm desperate for tomorrow,
 Like a desert in a drought,
We're pacing time we borrowed,
 Like the end rewards us now,
It's clever how we cower,
 Under the false pretense of pride,
  Mixing up the shallows,
   With the deepest corners of my mind

-June 2013 writing from rehab

The hardest thing for me not to rely on substances to survive is the lack of instant gratification. It's been an interesting process learning to accept long term gratification.

June 13th

I wallow through sorrow in meadows,
 On the outskirts of town,
Begging God for a dollar to borrow,
 Until our next conversation rounds,
  But I'm thinking forever,
   Kind of sounds loud,
& my ears *ache* for my heart,
 Who has heard it all now

-June 2020 the never ending fields of Wisconsin

I try to encourage myself to talk to myself out loud as if I were praying, regardless of where my spirituality/religion is at the time.

June 14th

I'm finding the sun in every crevice,
 Which feels kind of different,
  Almost *malicious*,
   To feel content,
Without the context of my past,
 Making it make sense

-June 2022 sunrise runs

When it finally stopped feeling uncomfortable to feel content, I knew that I had reached a goal I didn't even know I made.

June 15th

Teach me,
 How to feel normal,
  When we can't define the word,

Teach me,
 How to reach people,
  That I cannot afford,

Teach me,
 The cost of living,
  In a society of people not living,
But *existing*

-a broken spoken word

Throughout my journey the biggest obstacle I've always felt was being heard.

June 16th

Sometimes,
 I turn up radio,
But it doesn't drown out the noise,
I just line the bass up,
 With my stuttered heart,
  & use white knuckles to stay poised

-June 2022 on my last leg

Eventually the miserable drive home to go straight to bed was enough for me to make changes.

June 17th

I'm phishing for forever,
    & my lines finally gone
taut,
My bobbers drowning in the
water,
    Caught on all my restless
thoughts,
Like a kid with his first fish,
I'll beg for someone else's
help,
Then tell everyone I did it,
All by my damn self

-June 2020 a family that fishes

I never really fell in line with
the family tradition of hunting
and fishing.

June 18th

I'm running out of options,
 & I think the winds at my
back
I seem to saturate the
madness,
 Like the kids who sit in back
I've been overly unruly,
 Living out my dreams

-June 2022 train, train, train

I have to stop myself from accelerating the exasperation of options that may be viable if I just slow the *fuck* down.

June 19th

He taught me to stand,
 Shake a hand with respect,
He showed me how to love,
 Even when I'd forget
He spoke up when it mattered,
 Yet his quiet was power
I never realized as a child,
 The miles that he traveled,
In his mind,
 On his feet,
  Never a peep of regret in his smile

-June 18th 2023 a poem for dad

Grateful to always have had a good male role model to look up to.

June 20th

I'm dancing out of tune,
 To all my memories on loop,
  The scenes become rifts,
   & the words turn to notes,
Sometimes I hit repeat,
 Just to see if I see change,
  If all this love is pain unmasked,
   I'll let the rain dictate my path

-June 2022 2 step in my head

I can't allow my ears to hear the melody they want, just to reflect what I want my memories to hold

June 21st

& then the road turns,
 It splits in such a mischievous fashion,
  That my peripherals start to cry,
Leaving such beauty for beauty,
 Like dozing off at sunset,
  Just to be greeted on the rise,
& like the final scene of the series,
 There is no sequel left to find

-June 2014 rehab notes

This is a favorite of mine. So many forks in the road & so many wrong & right choices at the same time.

June 22nd

I quit searching for forever,
  & accepted each horizon,
    As never ending silence,
      Screaming from the sky,
I'll fly too close to the sun,
  Before it's all said & done,
    With a palette full of pride,
      That I'll taste with my eyes

-June 2013 writing from rehab

I've always identified with
Icarus & his story.

June 23rd

I have a tendency,
  To save memories,
    In lieu of reveries,
I can't escape

I'll save yesterday,
  For a later date,
    As I interrupt fate,
Today

-June 2016 Chippewa Correctional thoughts

Sometimes the best I could do was negotiate that I'd leave processing the past for another day.

June 24th

I'm salivating over the
sweetness of nothing,
 Like I'm 3 years old,
  Wearing cake for breakfast,
The timeless thoughts,
 Of forevers something,
  Will catch you off guard
when you least expect it,
& I think I've found it,
I just don't know what it is,
Rhyming in conjunction,
With whatever,
 I feel fit

-June 2022 I may be on to something

We have a tradition in our household that we do cake for breakfast on birthdays.

June 25th

I walk through an ocean of
eyes,
 Who by nature,
  Are required to pass
judgment,
  Before they even realize
they're doing so,
Which leaves I,
 Another sacrifice of society,
  That mines minds,
Under a false pretense of
truth

-a broken spoken word

Everybody judges, it's human nature, the trick is trusting humanity enough to let them make their own impression.

June 26th

Hazy skies,
 Remind me to breathe,
  I always seem to forget,
My lungs freeze in the heat,
 When my heart gets in the mix
I think I'm stuck fixing,
 What's probably not broke

-June 2013 Arizona breathes fire

When I start breathing with my emotions I am almost always bound to lose.

June 27th

First things first,
 I don't,
  want,
   Any sympathy,
I *want*,
  misery,
   Disguised as symmetry,
I'll let the devils dance this way

-June 2015 writing from rehab

Experiencing loss in a locked facility was beyond frustrating. In hindsight though me being there probably saved my life.

June 28th

I'm drawing up concepts on a canvas,
  That only I'm allowed to see,
& I'm fraternizing with a faith,
  That probes secular beliefs,
I've never been one to paint,
But I guess I just don't know,
 How to explain,
  Pain without picturing,
   Yesterday's dreams

-June 2017 Chippewa Correctional thoughts

Prison was the first place I was exposed to different religions. Watching different cultures & faith intertwine in a traumatic setting.

June 29th

It's like when you fumble for
your keys,
   At the front door,
     In the pitch black,
& you get that feeling that
somethings coming,
   It's almost loud,
     It's just like that,
Except the *noise* never turns
off

-June 2020 drinking like a kid
again

There isn't a substance on
this planet besides my truth
that will ever turn off the noise
I tried to drown out.

June 30th

I used to run with denial,
 That anyone would catch up,
I used to write the finale,
 Before the plot was even drawn up,
It's sensible sadness,
 We exaggerate in our poems,
In search of wholesome advances,
 But we keep coming up cold

-June 2013 the desert oasis

The most wholesome friendships I developed amongst men were trauma bond based. These also led to the biggest disappointments & sadness. Joy truly is sorrow unmasked.

July 1st

Sometimes I preface conversation,
 With anticipated error
  Like a prenup no one wants,
But in case this sale goes south,
I won't be liable for the cost

-July 2017 Chippewa Correctional thoughts

I've always had social anxiety, I've always felt like I have to warn others of the impending doom if I start juggling the words I want to say amongst my vocal cords.

July 2nd

I'm acting on the notion,
 That I'm better off alone,
  Like a bird avoiding winter,
   I'm letting my soul ride the wind home,
But the nest no longer exists,
 The trees all uprooted,
  If it's true ignorance is bliss,
I wonder when truth becomes euphoric

-July 2022 the next right thing cont.

Home is everywhere & nowhere, it changes & it morphs with seasons, with people, with everything that encompasses life.

July 3rd

The trees are reaching for tomorrow,
 Their hands outstretched,
  Begging for the flowers,
But they just miss the scent
These leaves always leave me
 To wage war against the sun,
It's *like* the darks finally leaving,
It's *like* the loves finally done

-July 2013 a forest on a mountain above a desert

If nature & all of its volatility can exist in relative peace, then we as humans can as well.

July 4th

I'm sputtering in neutral,
 & I can't afford the labor,
  So I'll just turn the volume up,
   & save myself later ,
I'm a favor away,
 From a debt I can't repay,
  Dodging sentiment for space,
   To escape the allure of yesterday

-July 2020 I might break down

Sometimes I just gotta turn the music on & keep moving.

July 5th

The memories keep drifting
 For better or worse,
I'd bet on the latter,
The obvious course,
 I have no horse in the race,
  I'm saving face for the
former,
I'm loading up on love,
 So I can recluse to my corner

-July 2022 betting on myself

I get caught in this summer cycle of letting myself receive & give love because I'd get so used to hibernating all winter.

July 6th

My faith seems to waver,
 But only with you,
Like it's on cue that I lose,
 Right before,
  The tools I've consumed,
   Repair the foundation I
confused,
So if you'll bend,
 I'll break,
  For the sake of avoiding,
   An avoidable mistake

-July 2022 chalk it up to the plot

It's easy to find excuses to break boundaries when I'm thinking with emotion.

July 7th

Too busy chasing a face,
 That I don't even know,
  Through alleys &
heartaches,
   The case has gone cold

-July 2013 writings from rehab

I chased every love I never needed. That whole self-love cliche is really that simple.

July 8th

I paved roads,
 Only known to one,
  I sold souls so cold,
   Under cover from the sun,
I forgot to wash my hands,
 But remembered hers' dirty

-July 2017 Chippewa Correctional thoughts

A cliche I love from the program of AA/NA is, "Keeping your side of the street clean".

July 9th

I feel distant from the
distance,
 Suffocating on whispers,
  Chasing nevers through forever,
   In an effort to miss it
I finally caught the wind,
 Just before the edge,
Regurgitating sweet nothings,
 Into each breath

-July 2022 post-run clarity

I like to run without a destination a lot. I stress over structure & I feel like letting go of that during something that is all about fundamentals & muscle memory provides balance.

July 10th

My own head seems foreign,
 As I ponder the rain,
  I'm alone with yesterday,

Feigning peace for desperate space,

It's a taste of tomorrow,
 I avoided today,
  So I sit with irony,
& let tears reign

-July 2013 monsoons ensue

Something about a gloomy summer day that has me dwelling on the past.

July 11th

I love every mistake I can't
hold onto,
 The void I'm left with,
  Bears the weight of mortality,
I'm a bluff charge from a
vicious predator,
 Sitting on a pedestal,
  I've always longed to leave

-July 2022 on the road again

When I was a kid I used to daydream on car rides that a bear was running parallel with our car, just waiting to peek its head out of the forest.

July 12th

I'm painting murals of heroes,
 I made up in my head,
  I'm frugal with the faith,
   I've mistaken for love,
I chase the sun through the mountains,
 Like a bug desperate for light,
Watching the melodies dance through,
 The grip I clench out of spite

-July 2017 Chippewa Correctional thoughts

I was always told to pay attention to those I didn't want to hear from because I'd learn something. Everyone has a story I can learn from.

July 13th

& then there was rain,
  & I know you'll say we needed it,
  But I'm not we,
& like a stand-off in the woods,
  Between hunter & prey,
We both sit,
  Watching smoke dance off our tongues,
Daring the other to breathe

-July 2013 writing from rehab

I can't let the chaos I've lived with become the dynamic of friendships & relationships.

July 14th

I paddle through ponds,
  Turn rivers into lakes,
    Until I am the commotion of
the ocean,
    Breathing in waves,
My lungs fill with goodbyes,
 I never comprised,
   Lost in a hurricane of nerves,
    I'm desperate to survive

-July 2022 we don't always get good-bye

I've always practiced speaking my mind because the cycle of life does not discriminate.

July 15th

I'm out pacing the sun,
 But I never beat him up,
  & mother nature nurtures,
   Even when we neglect her love,
Like waves crashing to shore,
 I just don't know how to stop,
& with each step I stagger,
 A corner of my mind unlocks

-July 2022 done before the sun

My goal everyday is to finish my morning self-care routine before the sun comes up. Shout of prison for the early wake ups they instilled.

July 16th

I keep one eye on the clock,
 In case the hours catch up,
It's hard to hear over the seconds,
 & these minutes push luck,
Like a guitar riff at sunset,
 I'm melancholy content,
  Using the sky as a canvas,
   To scribe the cursive in my head

-July 2017 Chippewa Correctional thoughts

I think it's impossible to completely live in the present, fully.

July 17th

What if the wind had a taste?
 Would you salivate?
  Watching your dreams blow
away,
Over rivers,
 Through mountains,
  With no way to escape

-July 2013 my first dust storm

Imagine if the wind carried all of your most glaring characteristics across its path.

July 18th

Sometimes,
 I watch the sun,
  Dance above the mountains,
& imagine the love lost in canyons,
 To faceless bandits,
  Out to rob you of your own mind

-July 2013 the Sedona sun

We live in a world where everything we hear is about how unsafe everything outside of us is when the real villain is just chillin' upstairs in our attics.

July 19th

I reach for my memories in
the fire,
 & retract like a child,
  Who's mother warned him,
   Of the inevitable pain,
    That comes,
From walking with insanity

-July 2022 Summers' heat

I have lived a life of trial & error, I still do, despite the cons it's where I seem to find the most growth.

July 20th

I always felt calm on the road
 I never really wondered why,
  It's the obvious notion of motion,
   That stills my eyes,
It's the melodies in my ear,
 That help me disappear,
  From the reality,
   That gets caught between signs

-July 2020 a summer of drunken roads

I love driving, I can throw on my music & go forever. Something about the constant motion that calms my head down.

July 21st

& then the sun set,
  And as I rised,
  For a brief second,
I felt the wind brush my face,
Like that day you rose with me

-July 2017 Chippewa Correctional sunrises

I always woke up for the sunrise in prison. It was so quiet, almost like a summer camp with the lack of state issued uniforms.

July 22nd

When I was 12,
 I watched my innocence
burn,
 I watched my dreams turn to
smoke,
  & draw swords,
   & have a battle in my lungs,
    My ancestors would of
sang songs of

-a broken spoken word

Processed trauma turns to art & I wish in psychology we focused more time finding the passion for purpose that is glaring during the healing process.

July 23rd

Sometimes I feel so isolated,
 Like I'm daring nature to enact,
  A law that reveals the humanity,
   I desperately try to avoid,
I'm soiling secrets I can no longer stomach,
 Hungry from an empty,
  I'll no longer leave behind

-July 2014 a fresh lapse

At some point I started feeling alone surrounded by people even when I was high. My mental tolerance for masking everything gradually became unattainable.

July 24th

I'm replicating emotions,
 Soliciting secrets for
seclusion,
  && I won't admit I'm losing,
  Until I'm blue in the face,
I'm watching rain cascade,
 Over all my favorite
memories,
 This storm seems to scream,
  I can no longer relate

-July 2022 scattered thunderstorms

Pride will deny joy to even the most suited of humans.

July 25th

To live is to trust,
 & I think we forget that,
 & to trust is to love,
 I've heard the hate can't
combat that

-July 2015 writings from rehab

The worst rehab ever taught me to trust even with the expectation of failure.

July 26th

& one day I noticed it all,
 The sun through the coffees steam,
  Rising behind mountains bearing snow
While I shoo away sweat,
 I realize noticing is a lost art,
  A lost expression of freedom

-July 2023 back to the desert

Much of my life seems to have come full circle, it's up to me to translate how it plays out.

July 27th

I'm breathing in melodies,
 That I can't quite recite,
Followed by tendencies,
 I've yet to rewrite,
  My cursive lungs fail me,
   Right when you begin,
I'm foolish with the faith,
 That I'll turn to at the end

-July 2017 Chippewa
Correctional therapy

When I get anxious it feels like the communication is written cursive & I'm struggling just slightly to translate it.

July 28th

I'm walking a tightrope comprised,
 Of every lie my eyes have cried,
  & I'm high above the city,
Where I can't tell breath from sigh,
I've never really had balance,
 It shows through my erratic absence

-July 2017 Chippewa Correctional's top floor

Lies pile up until the truth knocks them down. I've lived the polar opposite of how I do today, where everything I did was done in deception.

July 29th

& then the clouds parted,
& as the sun kissed my skin,
 I drew back,
Sometimes the lips we long for,
 Begin with a brush of discomfort,
Sometimes nausea interrupts us,
 Just as courage shakes our hand

-July 29th 2023 I found time to write

I get so caught up in my projects that I forget to just write sometimes. The whole point of this is to constantly put new words to paper.

July 30th

Sometimes,
 The canvas doesn't come clean,
  But still I paint,
Because what is art,
 But a once clean print,
  Made eloquently dirty

-July 2022 committed to art

All those cliche emotions people describe when they commit to chasing their passion is true & I hope more people find the courage to do that.

July 31st

I'm walking trails I didn't shape,
 With a melody of heartbeats I'd escape,
  In an instant if I could
I'm on the tail end of tolerance,
 Trapped in a collar of hate,
  That keeps getting tighter

-July 2013 writings from relapse

Often our subconscious puts us on an autopilot direct path to whatever we unknowingly set it to through our day to day actions.

August 1st

If you have a dream,
 You must protect it,
  & by that I mean,
   Relentlessly pursue,
    Every pointless passion,
Because peace will never peak

-August 1st, 2023 I found time to write again

I'm trying to never lose the core of my mission & that is to write. Sometimes, with so many things going on, the one thing that started it all, that helps, is the hardest to sit down & do.

August 2nd

I wear down my soles,
 Running parallel with my soul,
  Ironic how the desert heat,
   Doesn't touch this cold,
Sometimes I choose the easy rhymes,
 To remind myself to take the time,
To leave this all behind

-August 2013 writings from relapse

Sometimes it felt like I was doing everything right, getting the praise I always wanted but inside I literally felt no better than when I was experiencing the opposite.

August 3rd

I'm humming nothings,
  Just to silence the quiet,
    I'm an avalanche cascading,
      A lucid king turned tyrant,
I'm dancing a line so fine,
  The lies themselves sigh,
    Wading in the tears,
The oceans never cried

-August 2017 Chippewa Correctional thoughts

Everytime I read this one it has a new meaning.

August 4th

Slow motion commotion,
 Breathes chaos into calm,
  I'm acting on the notion,
   That you'll find the love,
    That leaves my lungs,
I'm exhaling papercuts,
 That never seem to heal,
  That came from the letters,
   I never meant to mail

-August 2017 Chippewa Correctional thoughts

In high-stress situations the brain releases epinephrine which speeds the brain's ability to process the events quicker creating the illusion that time slows down.

August 5th

I'm aware of each transaction,
 Like there's an audit on my soul,
I'm smiling through the sorrow,
 Because this deposit won't go cold,
Like a see saw in the summer breeze,
 We balance life with love,
Have courage through your shaky knees,
 Like the first time,
 Butterflies,
  Filled your lungs

-August 2013 the streets of phoenix

I find it easier to keep my spirits up when they are naturally low, than to maintain them high.

August 6th

I'm parading through the city,
That I never celebrated,
   & *maybe* that was my fault,
   Maybe the rain I chased
& wasted breath on,
Wasn't the storm I made it out
to be

*-August 2013 I was high before
I left the airport*

My perception on most things while actively using was negative & I don't think we realize as a whole how much that negative language affects us.

August 7th

I bathe in the calm,
 After the storm,
It's redundant when chaos
 Becomes the norm,
I'm forming opinions in the ditches,
 I used to reside,
  I guess I miss the company,
   The misery provides

-August 2013 looking for excuses to jump

Misery loves company & that applies to my mind mingling with my heart as well.

August 8th

I turn &,
 Let the sun reach up,
  To the scars on my neck,
A suffocating silence,
 That doesn't reflect,
  What hindsight reveals

-August 2020 going drunkenly through the motions

I was always afraid to say what was on my mind which led to scars forming inside.

August 9th

I hope one day,
 You quit waking up,
  In tears from lost fears,
I hope the face,
 You chase saving,
  Smooths through the years
I wish I could watch,
 That moment it sparks,
  But I've spent every cent,
   Trying to mend broken
hearts

-*August 2017 Chippewa Correctional a letter never sent*

If I ever have to get something off my chest I just write it out in a letter & stuff it somewhere. Eventually I'll find it & realize how irrelevant it was.

August 10th

Callused hands brush soft fingers,
 The touch of life is taken for granted,
  Forgotten in moments of anger,
Flagrant,
Violations,
 of *love*
Simmered in a summer

-August 2020 dynamics, dynamics, dynamics

In all aspects of life, we teach others how to treat us & vice versa.

August 11th

These backroads act,
 Like these ropes im against,
  & I can't finish this mission,
  With vision like this,
My knuckles burn white,
 With clenched fists tonight,
A menace of the memories,
 I wish I'd gotten right

-August 2013 floating through the mountains

Reckless decisions breed timeless memories, it's important for me to keep a hold on the risk.

August 12th

Someone,
 Send out a call for help
The hopeless fall,
 With another round,
I'll stumble home alone,
 At a hour,
   That turns moms face sour
Cowering in the corner from
another tomorrow

-a poem I found in a high school notebook

Teenage angst bottled up into a notebook.

August 13th

Spare me the narrative,
 I just put pen to the paper,
  I'll tuck every thought of you,
   In my save it for later,
I've found fortune favors,
 The labors of effort,
I'm missing a piece to this puzzle,
 & I forgot where I left it,
I guess I'm growing old,
 Through these bold intentions,
On the fence with my maker,
Dancing my way into heaven

-August 2017 Chippewa Correctional therapy

Sometimes it doesn't matter the other side's story as long as you're comfortable articulating your own.

August 14th

The canvas is empty,
 In line with this glass,
  These canyons cover
valleys,
   They'll defend till the last,
The cast is set,
 Across a script that's not
A plot thick with regret,
 Behind a mind that's locked

-August 2013 drunk in the desert

Someone once told me that it's my script to write in the end. Only I submit the final work to whoever is running the show.

August 15th

I sit insides of clouds of hope,
 My minds hazy,
  Eyes to the stars,
   I don't know how many
times,
    I've asked God to save me,
Not from myself,
 I figured that out
  But from the guy that hides,
   In the the corners of doubt

-August 2014 Winnebago County Jail notes

It's always seemed like there is a separate entity that's sat adjacent to courage in my mind that slowly leaks doubt the more time I take to act on indecision.

August 16th

Torn between street lights,
 They flicker with indecision,
There's a whistle in the wind,
 Loud in the quiet if you listen,
I follow the tune,
To the edge of the end,
& whisper sweet nothings,
 To no one again

-August 2013 meandering the tents of Phoenix

The absence of fear while high in a completely foreign, very unsafe area when now, I can't lock eyes at a grocery store without anxiety.

August 17th

The melody,
 Never really tuned to my
ears,
  My fears become eloquent,
   As the gin disappears,
It's wonder I made it to an age
I regret,
With lungs filled with smoke,
  Just to cover my scent

-August 2020 my skin is filled with gin

Ever look in the mirror after a long bender & notice the drugs & alcohol becoming a part of your body through blemishes & scars.

August 18th

These 20/20 eyes,
 Miss love hindsight spies,
  How convenient,
To believe in a lie,
 My own blue eyes construed,
  How lenient,
To confront a past,
 Before it passes it's last circle full,
  It collapses,
Under pressure meant,
 For diamond hands we buried

-August 2022 living through hindsight

Hindsight is a super power.

August 19th

I've always wondered why I dream,
 In broken destinies,
  Seeing myself on a pedestal,
   I've always longed to leave,
I'm fond of the future,
 But I forget the past is looming,
Another fool with some fiction,
 Planting melodies to bloom

-August 2014 Winnebago County Jail notes

The recurring dreams from withdrawal are brutal.

August 20th

My mind wanders like the
water,
 I just wish it'd stay current,
I'm an architect of disaster,
 Who's caught in the moment,
I preach loud in my silence,
I just hope that you notice

-a poem I wrote from outpatient (2011?)

When I wrote this I was loud in my loud & preached nothing of value to anyone.

August 21st

Take a piece of the pie & flee,
 The worlds on its knees,
  Listening for mercy,
   But missing the pleas ,
It's so ironic that we've lost it,
 In the middle of tomorrow,
  It's just aloha,
   sayonara,
& what more can I fit in my pocket

-August 2022 chaos ensues

At some point it started to feel like the world was slowly ending & I think that has a profound effect on art.

August 22nd

Sometimes a sunset,
 Is more than it seems,
  If you believe,
   In that sort of thing,
I used to,
 But I'm used too,
  Feeling insane,
There's pain on the window,
That we look out & see,
Memories we never captured,
 As we prepare to dream

-August 2016 one last fix

Any kind of lapse of healthy behavior to unhealthy began well before the actual action.

August 23rd

The trees seem to reach,
 I just wonder how far
& our souls seem to meet,
 When I notice the stars,
I admit it's not often,
My heads been down,
 Not in reluctance,
  But with purpose sublime,
So i'm signing my name,
 If I can find a dotted line,
It's funny how lovely,
 Life turns over time

-August 2022 sunset walks through my past

I wish the trees could tell us their story.

August 24th

I think we should go,
 Somewhere only we've been,
  Sins hand in hand,
   It's been so long since I've seen me,
& I've seen it all,
 The demise by which I fall,
The walls as they close
 & the curtains as they call

-August 2022 battling boundaries

One day I looked in the mirror & realized how long it'd really been since I'd actually seen myself looking back.

August 25th

It all comes around,
 In sounds of sharp *silence*
A *violent* idle,
 Along a buckled route,
  We lost time in,
Now my thumb,
 Sits on the horizon,
  By the side of the road,
  The cost of searching for a home,
   Everywhere but home

-August 2013 the Arizona heat buckles

I encourage people to be careful in getting caught up in the pink cloud of relocation.

August 26th

I'm reaching for ceilings
again,
 Take it how you want,
I fear its seeping again,
 My thoughts to my lungs,
I'm leaving like I said I would,
 I might never look back,
Just my thumb & forever,
 With dust covering my tracks

-August 2017 Chippewa Correctional chronicles

One time someone told me that when they get anxiety, it feels like all their bad thoughts are leaking into their lungs to stop them from breathing.

August 27th

I don't know what I'm doing,
 & in steps the beauty,
Foolish woes quit computing,
 & truly it's soothing,
I finally found today,
 Hiding behind my eyes,
  Fighting for a say,
   In tomorrow's hindsight

-August 2022 I'm still lost

Most of the time I have no idea what I am doing.

August 28th

Here sits the man,
 Weary,
  Weighing options under the moon,
Clueless to the plot,
 He just holds onto that dreaded page,
  Begging for the words to change

-August 2017 Chippewa Correctional thoughts

Observing middle aged men who put on a tough exterior while masking probably some of the most traumatic shit known to man is exhausting.

August 29th

The fork in the road is bent, ,
The horizon covered by dust,
 Bluegrass melodies,
 Bring alive my lust,
  For a better life,
  Of worry free must have
nights,
   Atop the world,
    Inside our minds,
     Signs of smiles,
      Crack frowning lines

-August 2013 wandering the mountains of Prescott

A lot of the time the path wasn't as clear as common sense would dictate & I think that's lost of the bridge between people who suffer from addiction/mental health & those who "don't".

August 30th

Man I love to run,
 Run from what matters,
   most,
I'll hit the coast,
 By midnight,
& raise a toast,
 To lonely lights

-August 2013 liquor by a streetlight by an ocean

Running isn't a bad thing, if it's helping to balance out whatever you're running from.

August 31st

My mind flutters with light,
My souls stuck behind shutters,
 I shut my strife off to love,
 I don't think I want another,
I'm fine inside,

 I *lied*,

But I'll find peace,
 In the fall of summer

-August 2022 I dread the end of summer

The end of summer always signaled the beginning of seasonal depression for me.

September 1st

I've found most decisions I
have,
 Come down to two choices,
Put simply,
 The *right*,
  Or the *wrong*,
   Both convincing voices,
I sneak annoyed glances,
 In a mirror distorted,
Trying to decide,
 Which shoulder to dust off

-September 2017 Chippewa
Correctional thoughts

When it becomes too easy for me to follow the wrong choice, when I know the right, then I gotta ask for help.

September 2nd

It's never been easy to be me,
 & I've never known why,
I keep it stuffed deep,
 Behind a California high,
Been away from my head,
 It's been the calmest of times,
Just palm trees,
 & love me's,
  Snow to sunshine

-September 2015 a love hate relationship

I sat in a victim complex like this for a long time.

September 3rd

I'm wasted alone,
 Stuck in a sedated crowd,
  Drunk off the dust,
   On the outskirts of town,
Tell me why we all,
 Follow our hearts,
  To a familiar fate?
That's the beauty of life,
 We all feel it the same

-September 2013 writings from relapse

Ironic that we spend so much time pointing out the differences in each other when so many of our experiences are shared ones.

September 4th

When the failsafe gives,
 Who's underneath to
support?
  Will the souls escape the
collapse?
The baths run cold,
 & the bloods turned blue,
Consequences,
 Of impatience relaxed,
I try to see through the fog,
 But I don't see any clues
To get back to a reality,
 I was so willing to lose

-September 2015 psych ward notes

Please, always ask for help if you need it, there is nothing embarrassing about it.

September 5th

From the top of the morning,
 To an afternoon snooze,
Cruising' through my
thoughts,
 Wide awake,
  What a ruse,
I've found foolish love,
 Gives off the strongest fumes
My oh my,
 I love the high,
  I get from you

-September 2015 drug induced love

The exciting love & the one I needed were not the same.

September 6th

It just doesn't make sense,
 When I see you standing there,
Silhouette sorrows,
 Sink like terror,
  To the chair,
Fair is your skin,
 Why won't it translate to us,
Just a busted mold of love,
 Cut by faults that line the mud

-September 2017 Chippewa Correctional thoughts

Love often doesn't make sense & I think the simple trick I always forget is to just let it be at that.

September 7th

The wind sneaks a melody,
 Through the cracks in the seal,
A faint whistle reminds me,
 My heads finally clear,
I let my mind regress,
 As the miles start to stretch,
When I finally come down,
 I pray I'm out of this mess

-September 2013 trouble in the desert

Call me crazy but I think some of the relapses I had were good for me at the time.

September 8th

The world will paint our eyes black,
 Just to cover the sun,
If you could get a refund on life,
 Would you shop for a new one?
  Or let the plot come undone,
   In the middle of never,
    Trying on none

-September 2022 what would I do?

Sometimes questions are rhetorical for a reason.

September 9th

I find time ironic,
 We all try to bottle it up,
  Even though we watched
what happened,
   When we tried that with love

-September 2022 can't reuse time

This is where that whole cliche that the world would be a better place if each individual did their part to do the next right thing.

September 10th

& one day Wisdom
whispered,
 In a tongue I can only
describe,
  As the very moment lungs
greet cords,
   The moment instinct
decides to survive
"Tomorrow isn't real"

-September 2014 writings from
an attic in rehab

I wish I had been able to
apply all of the words I was
able to construct.

September 11th

Some days I feel like an option,
 Who doesn't have a choice,
  I wish I'd courted patience,
   Instead I married noise,
I'm sizing up the secrets,
 To the life I've always longed,
  But it's hard to chase your heroes,
   When they were villains all along

-September 2020 drunken scribbles

I've idolized different entities based on my actions throughout different stages of life.

<u>September 12th</u>

& like the stars before dawn,
 Shouting out in disgust,
  How could something so bright,
   Put out the light in us

<u>-September 2016 my last time being dope sick</u>

One man's trash is another's treasure.

September 13th

Every ship has anchor,
 But how often is it used?
  It sits neglected,
   Void of touch,
Until the swell,
 Outgrows itself,
  Then below it goes,
The hero of the shores

-September 2013 Lake Havasu

Everyone, including myself, forgets about the anchor until it's needed. Everyone is someone's anchor.

September 14th

I was never bothered,
 By feeling this tired,
  It's another excuse
   I can chamber,
    Into an already loaded gun

-September 2013 trouble in the desert

I used to pile up excuses in my glass until I was forced to drink the contents or let it spill all over me.

September 15th

I wake up drenched,
 In a pool of regret
  Fed up with the mirror
  & what it reflects,
I bet my peace,
 Against the odds
  & I'm runnin' up debt,
At the pawn shop with my sense,
 Caught in the current,
  Of the river of resent

-September 2015 another last chance

There is a complexity in actively participating in self-sabotaging behavior, while simultaneously receiving sympathy for those same behaviors.

<u>*September 16th*</u>

I've wrote masterpieces,
 Who've purchased real estate,
  In an alley off Main,
The catalyst to a lapse,
 That might lead me free

<u>-*September 2013 writings from relapse*</u>

Sometimes I got lucky and the reckless decisions I made led me to where I needed to be.

September 17th

I'm silencing my critics,
  & I don't know why I'm choking,
  I'm dreaming in prison visitations,
With glass between my motives

-September 2017 Chippewa Correctional thoughts

Intention & motives are more important than the results in my opinion. This may be a hot take to some.

September 18th

I'm walking backwards with
my captives,
 & I can't meet them in the
eye
I think I've finally found
acceptance,
 I wonder when I'll admit that
lie,
I'm tomorrows favorite victim,
 Another number in the
system,
  Waiting for the dream I
ordered,
To arrive

-September 2013 high in the heat

I would always seem to capture different parts of myself & hold them hostage.

September 19th

But I promise,
 I'm full of love,
  I'm just tired,
The ignored are annoyed,
 Of watching a generation expire,
& my desires keep dying,
 In a mirror,
  Lacking reflection

-September 2022 tired

Sometimes I am more tired than I've ever been, even in some of my exhausting times.

September 20th

I wonder where the clouds go,
 When the sky needs space,
  The high road seems too
low,
   To designate peace,
I'm sick of leasing a life,
From nothing more,
 Than a slumlord,
I keep hoarding love,
 Like it will clean itself out

-September 2015 the basement of a trap house

Clouds look completely different when you're sober & I don't believe it has nothing to do with the eyes.

September 21st

Sometimes,
 I feel like I'm fading,
  With the fog,
Begging the sun to peak its
jaw,
 & rise its mouth ajar,
Speak sweet nothings,
 Under heat,
  For no one else,
   But me,
So I can finally hear,
Something I believe

-September 2022 & then fall arrives

Autumn in Wisconsin breeds a nostalgic, melancholic kind of vibe that really helps some people find joy in the subtle changes.

September 22nd

Sometimes,
 I start running,
Because I lose pace with my thoughts,
& the words I mean to say,
 Get lost between my brain,
  & my heart,
I get caught off guard,
 By the same mistakes I make twice,
& odds are I was conscious,
 Of the wrong choice,
  The whole time

-September 2022 I think my thoughts are chasing me

I run because it turns everything off.

September 23rd

It gets loud in my head,
Sometimes,
 I see no escape,
  Walking a tightrope,
   Exhaling fear,
    Accepting fate,
     Breathing deep,
      peace,
       lungs,
Just one foot in front of another,
No need to look down

-September 2013 high at 10,000 ft

When I was homeless in Northern AZ, I spent a lot of time in the mountains, they always gave me this false sense of bravado.

September 24th

Diamond hands,
 Confined under pressure,
  Bury them with hate,
Said hands,
 Begrudged by the unwilling,
I guess,
 It's better late than never

-September 2017 Chippewa
Correctional thoughts

I used to believe the ends almost always justified the means but I now believe that statement denounces the importance of the journey.

September 25th

These Nikes mark miles,
 I'll remember forever,
  In my dreams,
   Wide awake,
    Tasting views,
     With a smile,
This time doesn't make
sense,
 Like the smoke off my breath
Blowing hope to the cold,
 I think I'll always resent

-September 2022 crisp morning runs

During the fall of 2022 I realized I belong under the sun year long.

September 26th

I'll sign the dotted line,
 Without my eyes crossing
fine print,
Just to see the scenes unfold,
 Under the dark lights of sin

-September 2017 Chippewa
Correctional thoughts

The amount of time I've wasted trying to convince myself that the wrong choice was the right is astronomical in relevance.

September 27th

The right choice,
 Is quite easy,
  The wrong just has proof,
   That the right choice
   Takes effort,
A blind step forward,
& the wrong just takes
comfort,
 Wasted motions

-September 2017 Chippewa Correctional thoughts

When the wrong choice becomes comfortable I know I'm in a little trouble.

September 28th

They say love is blind,
It's more like a child peeking,
 One eye up from under the fold,
  Well past bedtime,
   Curiously mischievous,
    Surrounded by innocence,
     Avoiding being caught,
      When really that's the goal

-September 2014 writings from rehab

I think children's behavior works well for analogies to love because of the innocent intentions behind them.

September 29th

Soft eyes wear dark bags,
 Like vultures circling,
  Under heat so intense,
That the oxygen,
 Has to fight its way to your lungs,
& your vocal chords,
 Cower in shade
Begging the the sun,
 To let the moon,
Come out and play

-September 2013 melting in Phoenix

I remember days so dehydrated from the constant drug use & lack of will to drink anything at all.

September 30th

I let tomorrow borrow today,
 I can see it in my face,
  In the reflection,
   In the mirror,
That I used to wish,
 I could change,
I put band-aids over my eyes,
 To cover bloodshot lies,
I hope that keeps yesterday at bay

-September 2022 facing today

Once I got rid of the self-made blemishes, it allowed me to see my face for what it was.

October 1st

The path keeps narrowing,
 & like the arrow,
  Just before release,
The tension is mounting,
& the question remains,
 Will there ever be reprieve?

-October 2016 the chaos before the storm

I think I find a lot of cathartic release when I read some of these & realize where my head was.

October 2nd

It's like,
 When your mouth says yes,
  But your head screams no,
& when you finally get home,
 & notice your smile,
  & realize the mirror,
   Has been the architect of
denial

-October 2022 I'm my biggest critic

I've often missed out on opportunities I would have enjoyed because I was too nervous to step over fears' line.

October 3rd

I'm fluent in silence,
 It tends to dance off my
tongue,
Sometimes the quiet,
 Turns violent,
  & tomorrow gets,
Caught,
   In my lungs,
The moon still smirks,
 In denial,
 Of the crimes of the sun,
Weaving yesterday's sorrows,
 Into poisonous luck

-October 2022 together alone

Ironically, I think the most powerful connections are formed in silence.

October 4th

The ocean looks out,
 Over a world on fire,
  Wondering if the solution,
   Is as simple as it seems,
To quench such thirst,
With the horrors she holds,
 Teasing steam,
  With wave after wave

-October 2013 Fire in my desert oasis

The trick is trying to decipher what's really that simple and what's beyond my comprehension of complex.

October 5th

The hills dance to music,
 That echoes through the radio,
  On roads,
   That weren't nearly as rough,
 As they are now

-October 2013 Tom's Suzuki Samurai

Tom (4/19/2014) had this little Suzuki Samurai that he would take boy's up to mountains of Northern Arizona off-roading in. It also served as a shuttle when I got out of jail.

October 6th

I can't,
 Print these feelings on paper,
But if,
 I scribe cursive,
  I regurgitate emotion,
   In the only way I feel worth
it,
I feel,
 Like a turncoat to anxiety,
  & my mind,
   Says I'm weak to find joy,
    From speaking in ironies

-a broken spoken word

Writing, art in general, is the easiest way for humans to make sense of jumbled thoughts & emotions. However, it's rarely the first thing people turn to.

October 7th

& one day,
 You forget how to win,
  You forget the gatorade
showers,
   The subtle fist pump,
The way Dad's eyes light up,
 Mom's lips parting,
  Ready to offer up Ice cream,
For a job well done,
It's ironic we forget,
 What we strive to remember

-October 2014 writings from rehab

We teach ourselves how to treat ourselves.

October 8th

I keep switching dimensions,
 Like a optimist switching towns,
I keep happening upon villages,
 That leave me dancing with doubt,
  That the cities will ever get it,
   I'll probably always move around,
    Avoiding the street lights,
     & stop signs,
      I never listened to anyway

-October 2013 high from city to city

I kept searching for myself in different places, thinking the solution lay in some foreign climate. My choices made any truth to this search irrelevant.

October 9th

I wonder,
 If I replayed,
All the deleted scenes
 If it would hold up,
  To the picture,
I always paint in my dreams

-October 2022 reminiscing

It's important for me to be self-aware of what movie I'm putting on.

October 10th

I'm drinking rainwater,
 Like my ancestors,
  I wonder if they were
dancing too,
Watching monsoons,
 From the mountains,
  Wishing lightning revealed
truth

-October 2013 writings from relapse

I've only had the courage to dance in the rain one time.

October 11th

It's fitting,
 We sing,
  Of dreams
We don't achieve,
I'm seeing everything,
 In nothing,
& I don't think
 It's what it seems,
I'm feeling again,
 & I'm conscious
  Of each breath
Exhaling broken promises,
Until I quit talking to myself

-October 2014 writings from rehab

Pink clouds are universal,
they happen in sobriety,
geographical changes,
relationships and friendships.

October 12th

I'm searching for riffs that
make me cry,
 That melancholy cure my
sight,
  Of every last design,
   That the architect got right,
I'm searching in all the wrong
reasons,
For *something* to believe in,
For *something* to make the
fight worthwhile

-October 2017 Chippewa
Correctional thoughts

I have to be acutely aware of
my intentions behind things,
it's easy to fall victim to my
own ulterior motives.

October 13th

Sometimes,
 I feel like I'm back on I-95,
  With my thumb held high,
Trying to decipher between,
 The wind,
  & my sighs

-October 2014 writings from relapse

Short-term regret tends to lean towards irrational thinking for me, while long-term regret is usually rooted in changes in my belief system.

October 14th

I wish,
 I could move with the wind,
A weightless serenity,
 Of sainthood & sin
  Miracles to malice,
The balance is on the fritz,
Mixed signals,
 Turn to misread signs,
The quickest service of the
lips

-October 2014 a trap house off Cherry St

The most common manipulation is the manipulation of self.

October 15th

My reflection,
 Leaves with the ripple,
I gave up on simple,
Because
 Complexity,
  Grips the roots,
   Of belief
If you told me before,
 That this would be now,
  I'd of left you in my dreams

-October 2017 Chippewa Correctional thoughts

Prison forces a lot of analysis of core belief systems both in their programming & in the day to day environment.

October 16th

I'll bleach,
The white of my eyes,
 To hide
  My demise,
Even,
If the stars can't bear me
 I'll still feel alive,
  In the sky

-October 2014 a trap house off Cherry St

Art captures moments in time, sometimes those moments have been my worst but I am able to read these & draw reason from them.

October 17th

I missed the memo,
 To cherish these memories,
  I never,
So I'll lead with my right,
 I left my peace in the header

-October 2022 it takes two to tango

I've always been horrible & awkward at dancing on my own.

October 18th

I stagger,
 Into the party,
  Like a dog among cattle,
Well behind the rush,
 But never late on arrival,
I come dressed,
 Head to toe,
  Regret to denial,
I'll file you away,
 For my demise,
  On the morrow

-October 2013 writings from relapse

Have you ever felt like you're dressed in the worst things you think about yourself?

October 19th

I wonder if you miss,
 The flush of the skin,
  Binging on love,
   Throwing souls,
    Into sin,
The finish line is empty,
The spectators gone,
The spectacle we hide,
 Finds the right in all the wrong

-October 2017 Chippewa
Correctional thoughts

I think it's important to recognize & talk about the difference between love & lust in the current state of society.

October 20th

I wish the sky could speak,
 I'm curious its tone,
  The flow of its dialect,
   & the silence between storms,
The clouds seem to whisper,
 But I can never make it out,
  Ocean eyes peering down,
   On a world filled with doubt

-October 2022 Autumn leaf sunsets

Wisconsin falls can be so peaceful when you catch that 55 degree day after a storm so the humidity battles away the crisp of the evening.

October 21tst

The sun sets in Tucson,
 & so does my heart,
  Canyons & alleyways,
   Play a soft evening guitar
The wine always needs tasting,
 & you're more suited for such,
What a place to chase dreams,
 If you've never found one

-October 2022 Tucson thoughts

Places can hold the same about energy people can & I think it's important to address that with art.

October 22nd

The sun snuggles up,
 Like a blanket to the cold,
Each morning,
 Brings a layer of frost,
  Coating characteristics
charismatically,
I sold my soul,
 To the highest bidder,
  Bitter with regret,
   Whose mind withers

-October 2014 a trap house off Cherry St

Souls are the stocks of the conscious

<u>October 23rd</u>

I used to think heaven,
 Was a lot closer than it is,
Now I'm indulging a forever,
 That doesn't even exist

<u>-October 2017 Chippewa</u>
<u>Correctional thoughts</u>

Our souls facetime with heaven everyday.

October 24th

Have you ever,
 Snatched defeat,
  From the jaws of victory,
Hungry for starvation,
 Unable to make the connection,
  Between symptom and ailment

-October 2014 a trap house on Cherry

It seems like right when I'm about to win I beat myself to it.

October 25th

I lost my wonder in the hours,
 When I tried to track the seconds,
I left my patience for a sentence,
 I paraphrased in my head,
I hold hands with genuine,
 For a while I'd pretend,
That the destination was priority,
 I'd justify the mask at the end

-October 2017 Chippewa Correctional notes

Days turn to weeks, months court the years but it's minutes that don't make sense.

October 26th

& one day it clicked,
 Like heels in Kansas
& the tornado subsided,
 Like a fever breaking
Giving way,
 To the most beautiful backdrop,
Comprised of,
 Every memory I'd shoved aside

-October 2022 today it makes sense

Cherish the days it makes sense.

October 27th

All Fires,
 Die over time,
  But we remember the
smoke,
On our clothes,
 In our lungs,
Dancing off our tongues in the
cold
The old days start,
 When you don't
acknowledge,
  The new,
Pressing forever for leverage,
 Finding the nevers in truth

-October 2022 embrace the embers

Grateful for each generation of the good ol' days.

October 28th

I'm eroding,
 Like,
  Stone versus the wind,
I can't pinpoint forever,
 & I forgot when it begins,
  I'm slowly slipping,
   Into some corner of my
mind,
Begging my nerves to curve,
 An already graded outline

-October 2018 average college poet

Stone is strong but the wind always wins.

October 29th

Bright lights,
 Reveal weary eyes
  That have been on the west
Of one to many sunrises,
Kindness in random form,
 Curves doubt in passion
  But I'm alone courting cold,
   Without warmth to ration

-October 2013 the desert isn't oasis anymore

You'd be surprised at the amount of people willing to help if you ask.

October 30th

The tones,
 Tell a tale of fair love,
With fairy tale pink,
 Sprinkled across the sky
Tough is the sun,
 Who holds on to day,
  For the sake of beauty,
  For fools lost in a gaze

-October 2017 Chippewa

Correctional notes

The sun doesn't get the credit it deserves & the clouds seem to bully it away.

October 31st

I suspect the games fixed,
 But I'm still chasing the prize,
I buried my heart in Nevada,
 Right before the lights took
my eyes,
I file away a feeling,
 I always misguide,
  & tear down this wall,
   I've been meaning to climb

-October 2022 something about the southwest

Sometimes it's more efficient to go through a wall rather than over it

November 1st

Sometimes,
 I chase the orange of
October,
  Straight into November,
Adding kindle to a fire,
 That's barely even embers

-November 2017 Chippewa Correctional thoughts

Autumn is the perfect time for fires but they eventually go out

November 2nd

I thought about heaven today
 & the debt karma pays
I lost my breath,
 With my step,
  Towards the edge of okay,
Does fate follow fools
through?
 When it's all said,
  & the loves gone

-November 2022 & then it was

smoke

I always pay close attention to the moments that steal my breath, no matter how small

November 3rd

I imagine God,
 Was one *hell* of an artist,
But he didn't have a mom,
 Who would put it on the fridge

-November 2022 a mothers optimism

There hasn't been a person, place, thing or thought that wasn't flawed.

November 4th

I've been sleepless,
 In Seattle,
  It doesn't really mean much,
It's hard to dodge the rain,
 When Summer,
  Turns to Fall over lunch,
I've learned,
 Love is harder to receive,
It's human nature to give,
 But they'll have you believe,
  The flowers won't bloom
next may

-November 2014 I wonder who they was

History tells us the flowers still bloom, regardless of the words the weeds whisper.

November 5th

I might pawn away some sorrow,
 Come back again someday,
  When I can find a new tomorrow,
   To worry about today,
    When the wind hits me I feel hollow,
     Like an old tree on its final day

-November 2014 pawn shop blues

The best time to worry about tomorrow is tomorrow.

November 6th

I've been separating,
 From the nevers,
  That replay in my head,
Laying belly up in some office,
 Regurgitating nothings,
  To some lady,
   With a bunch of plaques on
the wall,
Framed validation in awe

-November 2017 Chippewa
Correctional thoughts

Popular to contrary societal
beliefs, that framed validation
is quite skilled in guiding
humans through healing.

November 7th

I *hope* you think this is about you,
I *hope* the relevance grabs a hold of your hand,
Right as you turn to go,
 & makes you question,
  How nerves,
   Brushing together,
    Like an artist painting a sunrise
     Could elicit a response so erratic
      Out of such calming colors

-November 2022 nerves firing

I've learned to both trust & question my nerves.

November 8th

I wrote a poem about it once,
 I described it so perfectly,
  It was like birds releasing,
   As the last syllable,
    Rolls off my tongue,
But doves bear the weight,
 Of sealing both fate & hope,
  In the same breath

-November 2022 recognizing balance

What a weight it must be to signify such moments in the life cycle.

November 9th

I often speak to my cats,
As if,
 They know exactly what I mean,
& with,
 Their mannerisms marking mischief,
I let their ears & eyes explain,
Exactly what I needed to hear,
 I guess I just need them to translate

-November 2022 conversations with cats

My most beneficial conversations are with canines & felines.

November 10th

I'm silently sneaking,
 Among a symphony of souls,
I think when I forget to breathe,
 It's just my own keeping score
I wish I had the foresight,
 To cherish today now,
Dancing through tomorrow with the devil,
 On heaven's favorite cloud

-November 2013 writings from relapse

I forget to breathe when I need to the most.

November 11th

& then I was gone,
 Striding with eyes now dry,
  & chilled skin flushed,
The puttering of butterflies,
 Meandering about my torso,
  Ceased to exist

-November 2016 Outagamie County Jail scrawls

It's easy to leave love at the door when you're locked in.

November 12th

My cat always stares,
Through the slit under the door,
I've always wondered,
 If she wonders
 If even she wants more,
This whole house is her life,
 But even I,
  Stare at the stars,
   Longing for,

What's just out of reach

-November 2022 Maya cat the queen

If you ever need to get out of your head just go chill with a cat & try to figure out what it's thinking.

November 13th

Sometimes,
 I sit in the shadow,
  Cast by the sun,
My little corner,
 Of forever,
  When I could never,
   Find one,
I got accustomed to darkness,
 Chasing the light at the end,
  Of the tunnel I said,
   I'd never enter again

-November 2014 a trap house off Cherry St

It's bad news if I find myself caught up in a corner of my head. I stop hearing everything & everyone.

November 14th

& then,
you *whispered,*
How dare you cradle dawn,
 Just to fall victim,
  To the moon's embrace

-November 2022 morning poetry

I always try to remember it's what I do when no one is looking that matters more than anything.

November 15th

I'm trying to find the context,
 In between,
  The sentences,
   That reveal the sentiment,
I've been avoiding

-*November 2016 Outagamie County Jail scrawls*

I wonder how much tension was built over the improper context & tones in letters before you could phone across the world.

November 16th

I hear screams,
  That could only come,
    From cords,
Woven with love,
& I remember dreams,
  That could only be painted,
    With watercolor from tears

-November 2021 post-therapy notes

I can't allow the internal conversations to contain raised tones.

November 17th

I yearn for the years,
I smeared across the wall,
It kind of,
 Calms me,
There is no fall without a rise,
No storm without an eye,
 Life costs

-November 2020 drunken scribbles

It's dangerous when I start using hindsight to punish choices I regret.

November 18th

I'm worried,
 Winter whispers,
  All the curses I mutter,
   Under my breath
I hope summer knows I'm grateful

-November 2013 snow in Arizona

I will never complain about the heat of summer to the snow of winter.

November 19th

When I remember then,
 I feel empty now,
  I'm void of happiness,
  Surrounded by,
   My happiest memories

—November 2020 drunken scribbles

Sometimes when I fill the void I lose grasp on the natural happiness surrounding memories.

November 20th

& then,
 Tomorrow arrives,
  On time with all the luggage,
   You were worried wouldn't
follow,
& like knees before rain,
 The ache pulls & pulls,
  Away from the gift of now

-November 2022 the view from a plane

I like to rewatch videos I've taken from the window of the plane, it's like being in the middle of the vast ocean 32k feet in the sky.

November 21st

I'm observing chemical
reactions,
 While embracing the results
  & when I finally come down,
   I'll keep it all to myself

-November 2013 high at a sober party

I hope I've gotten to the point in my life where I don't need to hold things in.

November 22nd

In the midst,
 Of all the chaos,
  I found truth,
   I think the noise is soothing,
I'm mute when faced,
 With tomorrows cue,
  I think,
  I think I'm stuck losing

-November 2020 drunken scribbles

I think way too much for my own good yet not enough for the good of myself.

November 23rd

Cold hearts,
　Meet humid air,
　　Soothing the tension,
　　　Of chilled tones bare,
Away from the world,
Away from my thoughts,
　Alone with the souls,
　　Who hold my heart

-November 2022 finding home

Forever chasing the balance of weather like the balance of my mind.

November 24th

It's funny,
 As time lapses,
  The pictures make sense,
Memories I hold dear,
 Start to fog with each rep,
Just a step,
 & then another,
  It's all starting to clear
I sit in love with my blunders,
 I forgot how to fear

-November 2022 a long winded run

Things always make a lot more sense to me when the only thing I'm focused on is not dying.

November 25th

The raindrops,
 Fall in tune,
  With a melody of hurt,
My worth feels wasted,
 On sentimental words,
Further down the road,
 I see the horizon die,
  I size up God,
   On these lonely winter
drives

-November 2014 my brain feels like slush

It's cliche but not allowing yourself to be valued lower than your true worth is important.

November 26th

I'm setting boundaries in my head,
 That I expect the world to follow
  & if I swallow my pride today,
   I won't have *shit* to do tomorrow

-November 2022 no use to only you

Boundaries are useless if you aren't honest with the expectation.

November 27th

Sometimes,
 I spell your name in the
clouds,
 & wonder aloud,
  How different now would be,
   If I didn't forget the sound,
    Of my name,
Dancing about your tongue

-November 2016 Outagamie
County Jail scrawls

I've learned the best way to
remember is to try to forget.

November 28th

I woke up grateful,
 After months in a rut,
  I was sick of lying,
Through my eyes in a mirror,
It's all still foggy,
 A bit unclear,
My only choice,
 To size up fear,
  Like the new kid at school

-November 2013 a random halfway house in Prescott

Change is best friends with fear & worst enemies with courage.

November 29th

It's ironic the logic,
 That falls behind love,
  A shove in the back,
   & I'm right back with the lust,
I finally mustered up the courage,
 To up & leave my worries,
  Waiting in a hurry,
   For the time to start working,
Then one day it does,
 & the world opens up,
A lucky reality,
 I pray I stay out of touch

—November 2015 Outagamie county jail kitchen

I often tried to speak the idea of change into existence knowing it was the opposite of what my heart was willing to do.

November 30th

How ironic,
  That the closet I left open,
    Holds all the skeletons,
      I worked so hard to bury

-November 2014 a trap house off Cherry St

Skeletons are only meant to be buried after a proper goodbye.

December 1st

& maybe it was my fault,
 Maybe the noose,
  That you tightened,
   The gallows you
constructed,
    Were originally built for me

-December 2022 post-therapy notes

Arguing over who built the gallows doesn't help the souls who are standing on them.

December 2nd

I hear "Jesus take the wheel",
 Going in one ear,
  & out the other,
The last time,
 I let someone else drive,
 I was in love with someone,
  That turned gray skies to
color

-December 2022 post-therapy notes

As someone who is not a fan of being anywhere but the driver's seat, it's important for me to sit shotgun sometimes.

December 3rd

The nice guy finished last,
 Only he wasn't always nice,
It took spite,
 To open some,
  Unlocked corner,
   Of some wasted mind,
A land of freedom,
 Restricted by his own design

-December 2016 Outagamie county jail scrawls

Everyone has dark places in their head just as there are dark places amongst the mountains the sun can't touch.

December 4th

But words,
 Are forever,
  & these are printed black,
The way back seems
impossible,,
 Almost hostile,
The bookmark glides,
 Across the paper,
Maybe I'll turn it tomorrow

-December 2013 Yavapai County jail notes

I could read my life away & still be stumbled on when to start the next chapter.

December 5th

The winter,
 Always comes,
  With a different *high*,
I'm stuck stoned,
 Off these memories,
  I can no longer find

-December 2020 drunken scribbles

One of the true unspoken effects of substance abuse is the ability to connect with core memories.

December 6th

& when that door latches,
 Somewhere between yesterday,
  & forever,
You'll forget every never,
 You forgot to follow

-December 2022 post-therapy notes

I've had the pleasure of watching people chase & grasp a hold of their dreams.

December 7th

I keep trying,
 To build character off
reputation,
  & I keep staring in the mirror,
   Wondering when the
wrinkles,
    Will catch up to the mask

-December 2016 Outagamie
county jail scrawls

I need to be aware if I'm in
line with my character or if I'm
concerned with my reputation.

December 8th

I self-medicate to erase,
 A post-traumatic stress,
  I don't even relate to,
I should be dodging fire in my dreams,
 Like the men I know,
  Who I relate too

-December 2022 post-therapy notes

Comparison is the thief of joy & also the thief of self-awareness.

December 9th

I used to watch love,
 Enter my veins,
  In such a hateful way,
   The devil really does dance,
    Just as graceful as God

-December 2016 Outagamie County Jail scrawls

The greatest gift we can receive is love, it's a shame we've learned to bottle everything up for sale.

December 10th

I facilitate conversations,
 That I'll process sometimes later,
  It's not that I don't care,
  I'm just aware I can't stay focused,
I keep renting out space,
 At below profit costs,
  I feel most comfortable,
   Amongst the chaos & loss

-December 2014 a trap house off Cherry St

It's ironically difficult to escape the lure of living in a calming chaos.

December 11th

Bid us farewell,
　As we stagger alone,
　Just some *souls* stuck in
sorrow,
Pretending they're not,
Praying to wake up tomorrow,
　But unplugging the clock

-December 2020 drunken scribbles

I cut off the snooze alarm, it was one of my best friends.

December 12th

The shades lifted each dawn,
 I was always met,
  With a rush,
That drew smiles on souls,
 I think I was destined to love,
Tough is the skin,
 Bronzed over with dust,
& eyes always seem sad,
 When you spot them come dusk

-December 2014 a trap house off Cherry St

When I left Arizona I'd often dream of it, location & intentions matter.

December 13th

It seems we're all witness,
 To the end of the world,
I guess it's bad business,
 To hope for more,
But I'll untie the rope,
 In the eye of the storm,
  & drift away to cope,
   Where the sun feels warm

-December 2022 post-therapy notes

Hope even when everyone else tells you it's a delusion.

December 14th

I sought out the sentiments,
 I lost in a midwestern haze,
I folded up my memories,
 Stuck them in pocket,
  Brandish my umbrella,
Just to protect you from the rain

-December 2014 a trap house on a farm

The fog I experienced on a chilly winter Wisconsin morning was the same I'd experience in my head.

December 15th

I'm chasing pipe dreams
 Through the colors,
  God used,
   To paint this scene,
The canvas is tattered,
 As my mind is worn,
  & I'm sore in my head,
   From the tallying the score

-December 2022 post-therapy notes

I used to keep score with myself & my subconscious in my head, how exhausting.

December 16th

Once again,
 I have my sights,
  Set on the horizon,
   I'm just wading out to sea,
Up to my neck in doubt,
 Hoping lies set me free,
It's funny,
 How chasing me,
 Brought me peace,
Runnin' circles round a love,
 I didn't want to face

-December 2013 fleeing Arizona warrants

Even amongst the chaos I understood self-love was a missing key to living an actual life.

December 17th

I'm severing the ties,
 With tendons I won't release,
My muscles slack,
 With loss of tension,
My diamond hands fall limp,
 Silent under the pressure,
  That's what I know I'll regret

-December 2014 a trap house on Cherry St

I've had such a battle with letting things go & as soon as I did, everytime, I regretted the time I wasted white knuckling.

December 18th

Forever ends tomorrow,
 If these words are never said,
I'll fend off the fury,
 We hurry to meet,
  & face the jury,
   We lured,
    To the front of fate

-December 2022 post-therapy notes

My greatest tool is having people in my life I can regurgitate things to when I feel like I'm teetering the edge.

December 19th

I keep using time as an
excuse,
 To excuse the indecision,
I hope that if we lose,
 Someone,
  Reuses our vision

*-December 2016 Outagamie
County Jail scrawls*

There is always an excuse for
it to not be the right time.

December 20th

Someone once said,
 Is it better to speak?
  Or to die?
The words,
 You choke back,
  Have a tendency,
   To save lives

-December 2022 finding purpose

Shared experience is a key component to healing humans as a whole.

December 21st

If I could go back,
 To the night I left,
  I'd do it quicker,
   Than the forever,
    I keep replaying,
     In my head

-December 2016 Outagamie County Jail scrawls

I actually wouldn't but sometimes emotion outweighs logic in art.

December 22nd

I've tactically acquired,
 Through trench warfare,
  Acres as far as I can see,
Now I sit here weary,
 Battle worn,
  Void of everyone but me

-December 2022 post-therapy notes

Be careful of friendly fire in the heat of the moment.

December 23rd

I'm calling someone else's
God,
 Asking them to translate,
  Someone else's love,
 Before,
  Someone summons sense

-December 2022 post-therapy notes

Love is a universal language that the universe translates differently.

December 24th

I'm copying honesty,
 But it doesn't feel right,
Almost forced melancholy,
You can see it in my face,
 In the itch I won't scratch,
  I won't let you see me fade

-December 2013 Yavapai County Jail notes

Lying doesn't protect the people you love.

December 25th

The stars look different from
the mountains,
 Everything just is,
  & the stars respect that,
I wish I could capture the
silence,
 As I watch it dance across
the sky

-December 2013 last look at the mountains

I try to be as still & present as
the night sky above a
mountain top.

December 26th

It's said the dead don't talk,
 But these days,
  Neither do the living,
So i trust the whispers,
 In the fog,
  With no idea who they are,
How far gone will we go,
 Before we're the era,
  Who lost it all

-December 2022 post-therapy notes

We live in a society of only being able to speak our minds online.

December 27th

Just a lonely fool,
 Juggling faith,
The first taste of love,
 Is all it takes,
Make up your mind kid,
 Times runnin' out
Find some of yourself,
 Keep it safe from the doubt

-December 2013 Sky Phoenix Harbor

I spent a lot of time arguing over faith instead of finding some in myself.

December 28th

I still in the wind,
 & shiver from the sun,
I hold onto bold,
 As grip fails my tongue,
Long & far,
 Away in song,
  I listen for love,
   Through the fog

-December 2014 either high or dope sick

It's good to have balance among my inhibitions.

December 29th

Painted eyes,
  Never catch the glare,
    Elated from the air,
      That sets life to paper,
Careful of the stairs,
  They creak with each step,
    & it's lonely at the top,
      So hold your breath

-December 2014 sleeping wide awake

I hope if I ever make it to what I consider my top, that I am anything but lonely.

December 30th

You don't remember,
 What I'll never forget,
  & vice versa,
Such a curse of human nature,
We don't realize we bare

-December 2016 Outagamie County Jail notes

I have to read this one often as I expect others to just understand my perspective.

December 31st

These days,
 Keep playing out in years,
& it seems,
 Every time I blink,
  Another wrinkle appears,
I find my finger,
 Pressing rewind,
On movies I've seen twice,
Wondering,
 If the good ol days are gone,
Or just beginning,
& praying red eyes find white

-December 31st 2022

The good ol days are whenever you decide they are.

Printed in Great Britain
by Amazon